WORTHY

A Memoir

KERRY TURNER

Cover design by Agazar
Formatting by Polgarus Studio

ISBN: 978-0-578-86968-1

For Matthew…

My son, my moon and my star

Contents

~Author's Note~

This is a true story told from my perspective. To write this book, I relied upon my own memory and dialogue with friends and family. I have changed the names of most, but not all the individuals in this book, and in some cases modified identifying details to preserve anonymity. There are no composite characters or events in this book. I did omit certain people and events, but only when they did not add substance or impact the story.

*Everyone who terrifies you is 65% water. And everyone you love is made of stardust, and I know sometimes you can barely breathe deeply, and the night sky is no home, and you have cried yourself to sleep enough times that you are down to your last two percent, **but nothing is infinite, not even loss.** You are made of the sea and the stars, and one day you will find yourself again.*

-f. butler

WORTHY

~Prologue~

A tatted-up middle-age man in black biker chaps greeted me at the counter. Both of his arms were completely covered in ink, even his fingers. He brushed his long salt and pepper hair out of his eyes.

"Can I help you?"

I pulled a crinkled piece of white paper out of my pocketbook and placed it on the counter. My hands were shaking. "I'd like to have this word inscribed on the inside of my foot."

"Okay. I'll be back in a moment. Let me go draw up some renditions for you."

I paced back and forth in the waiting room, glancing at the wall filled with hundreds of tattoos. *Maybe I'll see something else that strikes my fancy*, I thought. But I knew that wasn't a possibility. It had to be this word. This sacred word.

"Do you like any of these?" My soon to be tattoo artist said as he placed a sheet of paper in front of me. "Wow! These are awesome, but I think this one is exactly what I'm looking for. It feels right. It's very me." I pointed to the perfectly sized one in script that stuck out to me. "Ok, great. Let's get started," my new friend said as he led me over to the table.

I took a few deep breaths. I wanted to be fully present for this moment. This wasn't just any old tattoo parlor I was in. For me it was the shrine in which I would fully step into my power, leaving my past story about myself behind.

He fired up the tattoo machine. I could feel the vibration of it as I glanced one more time at my naked left foot. I choose the left because I wanted it to be placed on the side where my heart beats.

I silently called the spirit of my brother Joseph into the room. Nearly four years had passed since his suicide. *Stand next to me*, I requested in my head as I imagined him holding my hand.

This is my silver lining Joe. The gift of this mess. I lost you, my marriage and nearly my mind, yet here I am. I choose this word about to be tattooed on my foot to be my miracle. My great discovery about myself. It's what's been missing for me my entire life and I found it in the rubble of all places. I know this isn't something the world or other people can give me. I must claim it as my own.

Knowing Joe would appreciate my grand gesture I finished, *I know it's a little dramatic, but well, you know me. I take my healing seriously.* I could hear his hearty laugh from heaven.

A wave of gratitude moved through me. A couple of years ago it would have been hard to even imagine I would be counting my blessings for the wild ride I've been on, but as I lay on the table, I couldn't help but smile.

"Here we go," my tattoo artist said as the needle braised my skin. I felt him carve all six letters of the word deeply into my foot. In a matter of moments, it was over. Glancing down, there it was in black script letters. My one word. The energy in which I would choose to live the rest of my life embedded in my soul, cells, and now my skin.

Worthy.

PART I

THE WRECKING

All great changes are preceded by chaos

Deepak Chopra

~Chapter 1~

July 3, 2011

It's true. Our lives can change in an instant. In retrospect, I can clearly see the precise moment the person I was the second before it all came crashing down ceased to exist. Everything felt different, as if transported into a foreign universe where nothing is recognizable.

A phone call morphed me into a life I was not prepared to live.

The trajectory of my life was completely changed.

Just like that.

Juggling as many grocery bags as I could carry from my weekend supermarket excursion, I dropped them to the floor in a heap. A couple of jars of marinara sauce went rolling across my kitchen hitting a nearby wall as I placed my vibrating phone against my ear. "Hello?"

"Kerry!!!" my younger sister Kim screamed on the other end of the phone. Her sounds had an almost primal tone, a way I'd never heard before. The muscles in my neck and jaw tightened as I braced myself. It was as if my body knew I was about to hear something unbearable. Something that would physically, emotionally, and spiritually bring me to my knees.

"Joe hung himself!"

Kim's energy coming through the phone was palpable as she squeezed her words out in between sobs. As my body sunk to the floor in a heap, I swear I could feel the heat of her breath come through the receiver.

"Is he dead?"

I've learned not to assume anything about Joe. Maybe he somehow survived. Anything was possible when it came to him.

"Yes," she answered quietly. "He's dead."

Feeling my body go numb, it was as though my soul was being sucked right out of me.

At 31, Joe was my younger brother by 11 years. I had feared for a long time that I would receive this phone call that his life would somehow end way too pre-maturely in some god-awful way. My brother had suffered from clinical depression, bipolar disorder, drug-abuse and a mixed-bag of various dramatic events that had me always concerned about how long he would be on earth.

"9-1-1 made me go in the room and feel his skin to see if he was cold," Kim sobbed. "His eyes were open. His tongue was hanging out of his mouth, with drool coming down his face."

Propping my back up against my kitchen cabinets, I felt the handle dig deeply into my upper back. Slowly turning around, I gripped the handle tightly, as if that would help me not shatter. I felt out of my body as I looked around my kitchen searching for some sort of evidence that I was merely dreaming.

"You HAVE to come here Kerry."

I made my way into the living room and put my cheek against my soft plush beige carpet to be close to the ground, just in case I passed out. *Safety first,* I muttered to myself, hoping my internal motherly voice would soothe me, as I cracked a slight smile at the absurdity of it all.

From where I lay in the living room, I could see the groceries sprawled all over the kitchen floor. Crawling over to one bag, I got out a banana yogurt and ate it with the pure intention to bring some life back into my increasingly pale body.

Kim continued to beg me to get over to her. "Please, Kerry. You have to come."

"I'm home alone and don't think I can drive." An overwhelming sense of guilt rushed through me. "Let me call James and I will call you right back. I will find a way to get to you."

The truth was I didn't want to go. Not even a little bit. Running away seemed like my best option. Perhaps I'd jump on the next plane out of Long Island. Anything but return to that house, the one I grew up in where my brother's body hung.

My husband James had driven out to Montauk, Long Island in the morning to drop his children off to their Mom for the holiday weekend. He answered his cell phone on the first ring.

"Joseph is dead, he committed suicide." Feeling like my throat was closing, I got myself down on to the floor again, as if that would somehow hold together my rapidly fragmenting self.

*Breathe in, breathe out…*I told myself repeatedly recalling my yoga teacher's constant invitation to "remain in the present." I needed this precious tool now more than ever: *Stay low to the ground and ground yourself in your breath.* My breath was my lifeline and the closer my body was to the earth, the safer I felt.

"I'm not going to be able to get to you for at least two hours," James said. "It is Fourth of July weekend and traffic is really bad. You need to go be with your family please."

"I can't do it. I don't know if I can go," I sobbed. "I don't know if I will be able to go into that house with his body in there."

"Kerry, you have to go and be with your family and support them."

Support them?

Then it came out in a whisper, "What about me? I'm barely holding it together here, James. I'm on all fours in our living room, reminding myself how to breathe."

7

And then I thought of my sister.

"Fine, I'll go."

"I'll call my Mom and ask her to come pick you up," James responded. He obviously did not want to give me any time to change my mind.

James and I had decided before he left that morning to have a little barbeque, just the two of us, once he got home that evening. After hanging up the phone, I slowly walked in my kitchen and stared mystified at the remnants of what was to be the dinner we were going to share that night. Chicken and asparagus were haphazardly scattered on my ceramic tile floor.

I knelt slowly and closed my eyes. After what felt like an eternity, my body jolted me back to the present moment. My knees stung and were crimson from the tile rubbing against them. I had no recollection where my tortured soul had just escaped to. The out of body feeling I was experiencing was familiar. It's long been a coping mechanism of mine. When things get too much to bear, I check out. I'm not quite sure where I go, but anywhere but the present moment seems like a better option.

As I picked the food up from the floor, I knew the only way to make it through this moment was to allow my soul to transport wherever it needed to go to feel like it wouldn't be extinguished from the agony.

Now rushing to get dressed to head over to the house I grew up in, James's Mom was at my front door within the hour ready to chauffer me over.

The driveway of my childhood home looked like an episode of CSI. Three cop cars, one big police crime unit, and the coroner's van cast all of us on a set of tragic confusion. Police officers stood in the front yard and directed me to enter the gate to the backyard where my family and some of our closest friends gathered. None of us were allowed in the house, except Kim who was being interviewed by the police officers since she found Joe's body.

In between my numbness, I sobbed with disbelief while greeting my relatives. *Thank God Mom is dead,* I thought as I made my way through the crowd. This was the first time, I was relieved she wasn't here, which felt odd and freeing all at once.

Kim was extremely pale and shaky by the time she joined us out on the deck after being questioned by the detectives. Fear oozed through me as I watched her walk towards me. "Is your blood sugar all right?" I did my best to step up my support game. Kim's been diabetic since she was four.

"Do you need something to eat?" Following her around the deck of our backyard, I was like a mother hen desperately trying not to expose the helplessness I felt.

"I'm okay." Kim's hands were visibly shaking as she pulled up a seat with the rest of us.

Once James arrived on the scene, he went straight inside and saw Joe's body still hanging in my childhood bedroom. He's a retired cop, so I guess that history somehow gave him special police privileges.

As he made his way towards me in the backyard, I asked, "How does he look?"

"He looks dead, Kerry."

"Gotcha. Way to beat around the bush."

I pulled James close, hoping some of his strength would transfer over to me through osmosis as one of the detectives approached.

"Do you want to see the body?"

Oh God, please tell me I misunderstood his question, so I don't have to answer him. I looked at James, hoping he was going to make the decision for me. *Yes, I want to. And no, I don't want to,* is what I was thinking and feeling. *What if I crumble and can't paste myself back together?* I searched James's eyes for some sense of sane direction.

"Trust me Kerry, you don't need to see him."

That was enough for me. Feeling relieved, I felt convinced that if there was going to be any benefit for me that he would have nudged me to do it.

"No, thank you. I think I'm good."

It was bad enough I was going to see my little brother in a coffin over the next few days. I didn't need to see him here, now.

Father Donnelly, our Parish priest approached me.

"Where is he?" I choked out. "Where. Is. He?"

Father Donnelly looked confused. "Is he in heaven or in hell?" I clarified myself.

Being raised Catholic, suicide is not any old sin, but the biggest of all sins a human being can possibly commit. A sin of epic proportions. The big Kahuna of sins. A first-class ticket for your soul to be condemned to hell for all of eternity. At least that is what I learned in Sunday school.

I'd spent the past 20 years, unlearning any fear I took on from religious dogma as a child by voraciously studying metaphysics and spirituality. Before my phone rang this morning, I felt certain hell was only a place in our mind, just like *A Course in Miracles* taught me. God welcomes everyone to heaven, no exceptions. As I stood before Father Donnelly, resisting the urge to grab his collar, I didn't know what I believed anymore.

What if the nuns where right? Where the fuck is my little brother?

"I believe your brother is with the Lord." Father Donnelly took my hand. "Some people cannot find peace here in this lifetime and I believe Joseph was one of those people. He's at peace now Kerry."

I so wanted to believe him.

The police removed Joe's body from the bedroom and placed him on a gurney in the mudroom. Kim and some other family members entered the house and went with Father Donnelly to give him his last rites. Even though I couldn't see her, Kim's wails as she gazed at

Joe's lifeless body as he was about to be taken from our house never to return, pierced my soul in such a way, it felt like someone took a baseball bat to my heart.

As I sat in the backyard of my childhood home, I could see the same blue sky I was cherishing only hours before on my way home from the supermarket. Clearly, I was in the center of a life defining moment. Something horrific happened and I couldn't change it. There was no going back to the way it used to be. And, despite my utter terror and sense of brokenness there was also a knowing presence somewhere within me. Even though it felt hard to fathom, I knew on a soul level one day if I dared to look, I would find gifts from this experience. This thought alone, allowed me to keep breathing.

~Chapter 2~

Excavation

"Want a Xanax?" It was one of my cousins and the question was hushed like a back-alley drug deal.

"I'm all good." I proudly hoisted a huge bottle of Pinot Grigio out of my bag, displaying it in my hands like I was Vanna White. "I came prepared." Making my way into the kitchen I dug through a drawer to find a wine opener. I've never done drugs in my life, but I was not above using a bit of the grape to take the edge off this nightmare.

A couple of other family members saw what I was up to and eagerly waited for me to pour them a glass. "It's been a long freaking day." My cousin Lisa and I clanked glasses. "To Joe."

We made our way over to the kitchen table where my adoptive father Vinnie — Kim and Joe's biological father was staring hazily at Joseph's goodbye letter on the computer screen. Mom started dating Vinnie when I was two, they married when I was four, and he adopted me at age seven. I wouldn't see my biological father again until right after my fourteenth birthday.

Not sure about very much in that moment, I was sure about this; Joe gave great attention to planning his demise. "Please cremate my body and scatter my ashes in the Great South Bay," I read barely above a whisper from Joe's other note that was handwritten with instructions on a piece of legal yellow lined paper.

We spent our summers growing up in a small beach cabana on the Great South Bay in Kismet, Fire Island. "How fitting he would want his remains to be there. That was his happy place." I placed the note back on the table.

Vinnie and his fiancé Margaret were on a cruise to Alaska and flew back home the night Joe killed himself. He left a note on the kitchen table "went to the beach" so they wouldn't go in the room and perhaps find him still alive; hanging there. "He did the dishes, made his bed, sent a limo to the airport to pick us up." Vinnie rattled off Joe's rigorous last actions as tears streamed down his face.

After a few more sips of wine, I made my way into the bedroom where Kim, my cousin, and a couple of friends were rummaging through Joe's stuff looking for clues.

When my mother became pregnant with Joe we added on an extension to our house and converted the garage into a bedroom. My bedroom. Joe recently moved back home temporarily and was staying in the room. The attic was directly over the bedroom and had a rectangular shaped removable thin piece of "ceiling" that could be easily moved to the side to access the attic via a ladder.

Joe had removed the cut-out piece of ceiling and hanged himself from the beams high up in the attic with a thick orange rope. When I went into the room, the cut-out piece was eerily left open and pushed to the side. As I peered up into the attic my stomach sank and I heard Joe say in my head what he wrote in his suicide letter, *I've made many bad choices in my life, and this is going to be my final bad choice. I pray I find the peace I have been so desperately searching for my whole life.*

"Me too brother," I whispered. I made my way over to his dresser that had at least 15 bottles of various medications I assumed were his HIV suppressing drugs and whatever anti-depressant cocktails he was on. Picking up his Narcotics Anonymous book that was on a shelf next to his bed, I started to aimlessly thumb through it and took a seat next to a pair of his folded jeans. The scent of Joe's cologne was still wafting off a shirt neatly placed over a nearby chair.

As I made my way to the door of the bedroom, I purposely stood right in the spot that I assumed Joe's body landed once he jumped from the table

"Is this where he was?" I asked looking over towards my sister.

"A little more to the left," Kim answered. She smirked and looked slightly amused.

I adjusted my stance per her directions. "Here?" I placed my hands in prayer position close to my chest.

"Yup, right there. What the hell are you doing?"

"I want to see if I can feel his energy."

I inspected the end table Joe jumped from. It was a fine piece of dark pine that my mother had in our living room for years. It was shellacked so heavily that I could see my reflection when I peered down over it. On it was a little ceramic ornament that was broken from the force of Joe's body when he jumped off the table to his death.

The tchotchke was a mother chick tending lovingly to a nest filled with three eggs. My mother had bought this piece over 25 years ago because it reminded her of the three of us. Kimberly, Joseph, and me. The people she most cherished in the world. The eggs she watched over as she worked to do her best to keep us safe from cracking.

It now lay broken in pieces. Part of the nest portion was still attached to the statue resting on the table, as the other piece lay shattered on the floor. I felt the now familiar drop in the pit of my stomach, like a roller coaster about to go into a deep dive.

"I have to get out of here. I need air," I choked. Quickly I bolted out the side door to the front yard.

The sun had just set. The sky was still lit up with flashes of hot pink and blue across the horizon. Trees on our neighbor's lawn across the street stood like tall silhouettes in the sky resembling skyscrapers. They seemed to tower over our modest ranch home.

"James?" I walked around the front yard looking for him. He was nowhere in sight. I stood in the center of the front yard and turned around to face the house.

The house was a pale yellow, but back in 1973 it was a bright fire engine red when Mom, her new husband Vinnie, and I moved in.

"What the hell happened?" I whispered. The air was thick with humidity. I waited patiently for the house to answer me. It was as if the house was a living breathing entity. The sixth member of our family. I expected it to burst into tears along with me in recognition of this unbelievable horror. I wanted it to wrap its arms around me and tell me everything was going to be okay. That I was going to be okay. That every joy and horror that ever occurred in that house was a part of a greater plan that I just didn't understand or at least didn't understand, yet.

As I stood on the front lawn that evening, never could I have imagined this moment—this soul crushing moment—would be the catalyst for such profound transformation. Within a few years, I would discover what had been missing for me my entire life. A deep sense of worthiness.

My transformation would not be instantaneous. It would not be linear. It would not be neat or pretty. My healing would happen in layers. A complete breakdown, a diagnosis of PTSD, a deep look into my past, and a divorce from James would bring me to my knees. Allowing myself to be swallowed by the darkness would be necessary to find light I never experienced before.

Three years after that horrible night, I would find myself entrenched in a darkness that I didn't know how to get out of. Desperate for relief, I booked a session with a Shaman.

"Do you know what is unique about you and what you bring to relationships and the world?" the Shaman asked.

"Um, my ability to connect to people?" I was pretty sure I had no clue where he was going with this.

"No!" My body tensed as he raised his voice. "It's your unique expression of love. No one else in the world brings what you bring. You do not value your unique expression of love. You do not OWN how worthy you are."

His choice of words and the way he said this truth landed deeply within me. As if awakened from a very deep sleep. My entire life I had been moving about the world as if I had no worth. As if my presence did not add value to people's lives.

I've heard many people say the Universe first throws pebbles to awaken us to see what is not working in our lives. If that doesn't do it, it will toss a few bricks our way. And when all else fails a wrecking ball experience may present itself to really shake us awake.

Joe's suicide was my wrecking ball.

~Chapter 3~

Grief Expert

"You've GOT this." I was staring into the mirror rattling off a laundry list of "evidence" that I had collected that I would be able to get through the day of Joe's funeral and beyond.

"You are an 'expert' at this grief thing, Kerry. You've taken enough workshops for the entire population of Manhattan and have read enough books on personal development to fill a public library."

Though I had developed a very successful sales career in electronics, I recently decided something was missing. In two months, I would be graduating from Coach U, one of the largest coaching schools in the world, with a Life Coach certification. To further hone my expertise and skills, I was in the middle of coaching a group of men and women in a 90-day leadership program for a company that does transformational workshops where I was once a student. Neck deep in personal development work, I felt perfectly poised to make it through this mess fully intact.

Still a thread of doubt ran through me. Would I be able to keep the anxiety that plagued me since I was a child at bay? Would my sense of inner awkwardness rise to the surface and reveal itself as I stood greeting guests at the funeral parlor?

By the time I was ten, I would experience daily episodes of complete and utter dread for no apparent reason. Accompanied by a choking sensation and feeling out of my body, it felt like someone had put a pillowcase over my head and wouldn't let me free. At the time I didn't know I was having anxiety attacks and vacating my body to feel safe. I just thought that there was something terrible wrong with me, like my DNA was botched or something. Inherently, I felt young girls were supposed to be carefree and adventurous. Inside my mind and body, I was clearly neither.

Everyone around me appeared more confident. I didn't feel like I was good at anything. Trying to hide my insecurities made me feel more anxious. All my girlfriends seemed to have some sort of special talent. They could sing, dance, play sports, get straight A's, or look pretty, just standing there. Me, not so much. I was fairly certain God skipped me when he was handing out special gifts and I was going to have to work really hard for other people to think I had anything going for me.

As I continued to get ready for the wake, I took a few more deep breaths attempting to keep the inner monsters from the past away. I thought of my mother Patty who I lost to breast cancer when she was 54, nine years before Joe's death. Eleven weeks after Mom, I lost my maternal grandmother Philly, also to cancer, hence my declaration that I'm an expert at "the grief thing."

Mom married my biological father in 1968. I was born a little over a year later. My father was in the Army and stationed in Germany at the time of my birth. An ocean between us. Emotionally, the gap would never close. Our relationship, or lack of, would eventually reveal itself to be a major source of my worthiness issues.

Mom and I flew over to be with my father in Germany when I was a few weeks old. She hated it, so our tenure overseas would only last several months. They were officially separated by the time I was 15 months old. I have no recollection of ever being a family. Back in the states, we moved in with Grandma Philly. Like sisters Mom and

I shared a bedroom until the day she married Vinnie.

Losing my mother was like losing my soulful compass. For most of my 33 years I got to be with her, I felt like more of an extension of her, rather than my own individual.

Mom used to sing the Ann Murray song "You and me against the World" to me as if it were our personal anthem. *"When all the others turn their backs and walk away, you can count on me to stay,"* she would croon with her Edith Bunker type voice. Her warm hands would reach for mine, filling my heart with appreciation that someone could love me that much.

After Kim and Joe were born, she would let me play hooky occasionally to help me feel special since I didn't have her all to myself anymore. She had a wonderful gift of making all three of us feel like we were her favorite child. When she uttered the words, "let's go to McDonald's for breakfast and then shopping…just you and me," I knew for sure I was about to have a magical day.

When Mom was diagnosed with breast cancer at 48 (I was 28 at the time), it felt like someone sawed me in half. She took me into her bedroom the day I arrived back home from my first big business trip for a new job. Removing her shirt and bra, she lifted her arms over her head revealing a huge dent in her left breast. "See?" Then she held up her mammogram film (this was way before digital was a reality) by the window. "This is the tumor," she said. Feeling like the lump in my throat might choke me, I remained silent as I nodded pretending like I knew what I was looking at in the films.

The fear of what my world would be like without her was so paralyzing, Joe had to hold me up in the elevator at the hospital the day of her first mastectomy. "One foot in front of the other K," he said. We moved in slow motion down the hallway through what felt like quicksand. Both of my hands held Joe's left arm in a vice grip, just to reach her room. Though Joe was eleven years my junior and the youngest in the family, he many times made gestures of support like this to me and Kim as if he were the oldest. The sight of Mom on a morphine drip drained every last drop of energy that remained in me and Joe quickly whisked me out of the hospital so I wouldn't need a room myself.

Equalizing in our new reality, I was able to quickly get it together to support her. "Kerry!" Mom called out my name from the bathroom three weeks after her first chemo treatment. My entire body tensed as I slowly opened the door and found her pulling a massive fist full of hair out. The floor was covered with her blond locks.

"It's going to be okay Mom." Kneeling down on my hands and knees to pick her hair up from the floor as she sobbed on the toilet, I threw it all in the garbage and slammed the lid down quickly so she didn't have to look at the substantial amount she lost within minutes.

Our relationship shifted that day.

Beyond supporting her with the cancer, she would call me up for advice regularly. "Sometimes I feel like you are the parent and I am the child," she said. We were chatting on the phone about a challenge she was having with a friend. Struck by her statement, I realized I was finally becoming my own woman. Separate from her. My own being. Not only did she recognize it, but she supported it as if she knew on a visceral level that soon I would need to navigate the world without her.

Both Mom and Gram had a deep faith in God. Raised Roman Catholic, I couldn't totally avoid the guilt and shame that comes along with that gig, but they instilled in me a *knowing* that God was someone I could count on and not fear. *There really must be something to all this spiritual stuff,* I would think to myself as a young girl watching them caress their Rosary Beads. Their devotion made them appear lit from within, as if those pretty beads gave them some sort of mystical superpowers.

Wanting a piece of that for myself, my relationship to the divine became a focal point in my life by the time I was eight. After Grammy taught me how to say the rosary and Mom explained all the mysteries and miracles to mediate on while reciting it, I set out to buy my own magical beads. "I'll take the pink ones." I handed over my money to the clerk in the church store, stuffing the holy gems into my pocket hoping they would bring me the comfort they seemed to bring Mom and Gram.

Since Mom and I lived with Grammy in my early years we had an extra special bond. "You're my fifth baby," Gram would say. Lovingly, she would cup my face with her hands, letting me know she counted me as one of her own children.

Gram taught me the fine art of shopping. Weekly visits to Gimbels was a staple of my childhood. We bought my first bra there without my mother knowing and would rummage through the discounts in the cellar area for hours.

Her style was unique. She dressed as if she just walked out of a Partridge family episode for decades, wearing the same quirky pants suits over and over. The only makeup she wore was occasional bright red lipstick that stood out against her olive skin and silver hair.

One of Gram's favorite phrases was, "Every time you open your mouth Kerry, I open my pocketbook." It wasn't far from the truth. In addition to co-signing my first car loan, Grammy was generous with the multiple twenty-dollar bills that always seemed to fly out of her wallet and into my pocket when I visited, which was often. Her presence was a safe space and I would show up on her doorstep unannounced just to spend time hanging out in her living room to chat about life.

One of the greatest gifts of our relationship was that I felt seen by her. I never had to put up a front. I knew on a soulful level she loved me completely even when I wasn't at my best. Without even so much as a "Hello," she would growl when I showed up at her house and I was late on my car payment, "Pay the damn bill Kerry!" In the next minute, she would drop the subject like it never happened, grabbing my hand to connect.

Gram also was the only person who ever witnessed me taking my self-hatred out on myself when I was about 11. I can't remember what I was upset about, I just remember the overwhelming feeling of wanting to be better. More enough. Less awkward and afraid. Picking up the pink Aqua Net hairspray on my dresser in my bedroom, I begin to violently beat my right hip with the can until purple bruises came to the surface of my skin. I didn't know Gram was visiting and was outside my bedroom door listening.

She knocked and I threw the can to the floor. "I heard what you were doing." Gram picked the can up off the floor, her eyes wide with concern. "What's the matter baby?"

I didn't answer, because I didn't know. There were no words yet to name it.

Mom and Grandma Philly were the two closest people to me in the world. As hot tempered as each woman would behave at times, I considered them to be my safety nets, my lights at the end of the tunnel, and my north stars all wrapped up into one.

If I could make my way through that tremendous loss 11 weeks apart and feel whole again, I could make it through anything.

I could see the sadness in my own eyes, almost not recognizing myself. *Who am I, now that this has happened?* I thought. I felt the familiar feeling of having an elephant sitting on my heart. *Is there a short cut through this pain? Will I ever feel at peace?*

Intuitively I knew there was no short cut, but I was still fighting to hold it all together at that point. As I walked up to the funeral home, my knees were knocking together so hard I swear you could hear them from blocks away. Realizing no matter what I had already experienced, no matter how educated I was on personal development, no matter how much evidence I had accumulated over the years that I was resilient; moving through this tragedy was going to be a journey unlike any other I have ever taken. Feeling like I was dropped in the middle of the desert with no water or GPS, I took a deep breath and made my way inside.

And then it happened.

I saw Joe in his coffin. Uncontrollable sobs fell out of me like nothing I had ever experienced before.

My entire body was wracked with grief. I held in my sorrow when my mother and grandmother died. I tried to control it, to take charge of it, and tell it where to go. But nine years later, as I sat there at Joe's wake, I couldn't put a lid on what I was feeling.

I must have been a sight. The funeral home employees were running around in search of a chair and tissues. "Here Miss, please sit!" One of the employees guided me into a seat not seeming to notice me shake with grief.

I looked up and James was standing in front of me. His face was flushed, his eyes were brimming with tears. "I can't stand to see you like this." It was the first and only time I think I ever saw fear in his eyes. In retrospect, I wish I had the courage to just fall apart in his arms. Maybe it would have softened the wall that quickly would build between us, allowing him to see the real state of where I was at. Instead, I soldiered up and tried to act strong in fear my current emotional status would be way too much for any other human to handle.

Once I was steady on my feet, I went up to my brother's coffin. Soon my sister Kim was next to me gazing at Joe's body.

"Damn, he looks good. He may be the best-looking dead person I've ever seen, in fact." I was terrified of how he was going to appear since he basically strangled himself to death and had an autopsy.

With an out-of-place grin, Kim replied, "The little shit probably exfoliated before he hung himself."

We looked at each other and busted out laughing so loud I'm sure we raised an eyebrow or two. Because as absurd as that may sound to people that someone would make sure they were well-coiffed before they killed themselves, both of us knew that was not out the realm of possibility when it came to Joe.

Hundreds of Joe's friends came over to comfort us at the wake and funeral and posted poignant memories of Joe on *Facebook*. We didn't even know most of these friends existed. In many ways, many pieces of my brother's life remained and continue to remain a mystery.

As I looked around the packed funeral parlor many things about Joe became crystal clear. The most obvious was how many lives he touched with his gregarious, quirky, and lovable soul. The night of his wake his deep infectious laugher was mentioned over and over by the strangers that greeted me at his casket. We all agreed his mischievous giggle could be felt right down to the toes of anyone within earshot of his unique expression of joy.

One of Joe's unknown friends called the funeral parlor asking if he could sing the *Ava Maria*, one of Joe's favorites, at the funeral. Even though we weren't quite sure what to expect, or if this person could even carry a tune, Vinnie said yes.

When this man opened his mouth, the entire Church turned around to see where this amazing operatic voice was coming from. It turns out Joe's friend was a tenor at *St. Patrick's Cathedral* in New York City.

As the music filled the church, it felt like angels were descending upon us. Everyone's eyes were moist with tears including the man singing as he belted out the *Ava Maria* with such emotional intensity and passion, every note he sang permeated our collective souls.

At that moment, I imagined my brother legs crossed, sitting atop his coffin looking up to the balcony where his friend was singing to all of us, most of all from where he was singing to Joe. I imagined Joe looking quite pleased at the beauty of the moment, despite our pain, and feeling all the love celebrating his spirit.

The darkness that overtook him extinguished.

Only light remained.

~Chapter 4~

Crazy Time

When Mom passed away, I couldn't believe how the whole rest of the world kept on going when I felt like mine was falling apart.

Within days after she passed, I walked into the local supermarket and felt this overwhelming urge to walk up to strangers while I was shopping and say, "My mother just died and here we are doing something as mundane as buying milk and bread. *How crazy ass is that?*"

I would imagine a kind looking woman, a few decades older approaching me as she tossed a roll of toilet paper into her cart while mine and Mom's Anne Murray anthem played over the loudspeaker in the store. *"And when one of us is gone...and one of us is left to carry on. Well then remembering will have to do. Our memories alone will get us through. Think about the days of me and you. You and me against the world."*

Grabbing my hand, she would look deep into my eyes and say sweetly, "The entire world should stop spinning until you catch your breath. Right, Honey?"

"Yes!" I would reply, ecstatic someone understood me. "I'm so glad you see it my way, let's press pause!" We would then high-five, hug, and I would be allotted the time needed to heal without having to deal with the "ins and outs" of everyday life. *If it were only that easy.*

I sat at my desk reminiscing about my entry back into the public that day, feeling grateful for the reminder that life does, indeed, go forward, even within the painful moments.

I trusted that this extra week off from work after Joe's funeral would support me to enter the world in a peaceful, yet powerful way. Hopefully I'd feel *saner* this time. My instincts were telling me to just "be." I thought if I didn't move a muscle, perhaps I'd be given some sort of supernatural ability to paste myself back together within a few days.

The lanky Willow tree in my backyard on Long Island became my new constant companion. Its statuesque height and glowing green leaves gave it a commanding presence. It emanated a healing energy that soothed me, as if God were within the branches towering over me. I've always loved being with nature, particularly at the beach. Feeling the elements around me at this time brought me powerful moments of connection to the divine like I've never felt before.

As I sat in the shadow of my "Healing Tree" by day, sipping my coffee, I would stare up at it imagining it was telepathically communicating restorative messages to me. I would visualize different creatures simultaneously roaming about the earth as I sat beneath my tree. I imagined the giraffes sauntering around Africa, the whales swimming in the ocean off Antarctica, and the beautiful red cardinals swirling around in my backyard. I knew for certain I was a part of an energy much bigger than myself and the situation I now found myself in. It comforted me to feel deeply connected. *I am just a speck of this universe, and yet I contain all the universe inside of me.*

At night, I would sip a glass of Pinot Grigio in its shadow in a white Adirondack chair as the sun set, placing a blanket loosely over my legs if there was a chill in the air, praying for the pain I felt in my heart to cease long enough so I could sleep.

Night after night, I sat in front of my new companion watching the sky turn a dark azure blue. Gazing up at the stars I'd try to feel my brother's spirit around me, looking for some sort of sign that he was still with me. During the daytime, every brown-eyed bird or rabbit that happened by me gave me the opportunity to start a conversation: "Joe is that you? Are you finally at peace?" I whispered to a bunny that emerged from a small bush. "Give me something to work with brother. I'm talking out loud to small furry animals for God's sake!"

If the bird or rabbit so much as blinked, I wanted to believe my brother was sending me some sort of message to comfort me and let me know he was okay, but I wasn't certain about anything at that point.

Three days after Joe passed, I felt his presence for the first time. This gave me a glimmer of hope that Father Donnelly wasn't placating me with his theory Joe was in heaven. The message was simple. The book I was about to write was no longer going to be a personal development book, but a memoir containing both of our stories.

A Memoir? I don't know the first thing about writing memoir Joe, I thought as I sipped my coffee outside. Without further contemplation, I whispered into the wind, "Ok, I'll do it, but I'll need your help brother."

And then he went silent. No longer being able to feel his energy, I became obsessed with looking for signs his spirit was with me.

Right before Mom had passed, I asked her to "send me a sign once you get to the 'other side' to let me know you are well." Within minutes of her last breath, I looked out a window and saw a tiny blue butterfly hovering around a lavender hydrangea bush and instantly felt certain that it was my sign from Mom. The butterfly was the same color as her eyes.

Joe was being more elusive. My fear of where he was persisted. Could I trust the message I heard three days after he left us? Was I making stuff up to feel better? At this point, I didn't know. I needed more evidence.

One rainy morning, I sat at my desk using Google to refresh myself on everything written about "the stages of grief" in a premature attempt to quickly move through all of them at warp speed. Feeling better as soon as possible became my *project de jour.*

According to Elizabeth Kübler Ross, the author of *On Death and Dying,* there are five stages of grief. Denial, anger, bargaining, depression, and acceptance.

I was bound and determined to slide through all of them very quickly. Most important to me at the time was to make a beeline to acceptance. Going through this process felt terribly inconvenient for me and I was as furious as I was confused.

My phone rang as I typed away on my keyboard. On the other end was the detective that handled the investigation into Joe's death. "I wanted to let you know there were no drugs or alcohol in your brother's system at the time of his death."

"Really?"

"Yes, really. Just a little Zoloft in his liver

Feeling a mix of surprise, relief, and disappointment, I exchanged a few pleasantries with the detective and hung up. *My God, he was completely sober when he did this,* I thought as my uneasiness grew.

Continuing my Google search, I gingerly typed the phrase *"when a loved one commits suicide"* on the keyboard of my laptop, becoming anxious about what would show up on the screen.

Quickly, I realized I was now what is considered a "survivor" of suicide; defined as "a person that has lost someone to suicide, is grieving and struggling to understand." According to the *American Association of Suicidology,* for every suicide, there is an estimated six or more "survivors."

"Yup! I guess that would be me," I said to my computer screen, "a survivor," now choking on the words glaring back at me.

According to the *National Institute of Mental Health,* over 47,000 people commit suicide in the United States yearly (CDC 2020), with 90% of these people suffering from a mental disorder like bipolar, depression, drug or alcohol abuse, or a combination of these afflictions.

"Makes sense. That's what Joe's state of health was before he ended it." I continued to bang away at my keyboard collecting my data and attempting to make some sort of sense out of Joe's senseless act.

I read article after article about what it meant to be a suicide "survivor." One "fact" mentioned over and over was this: According to the American Psychiatric Association's "Diagnostic and Statistical Manual of Mental Disorders" the trauma of losing a loved one to suicide is ranked as *catastrophic* on par with a concentration camp experience.

After reading this piece of data at least ten times, I couldn't keep silent. "Geez! I'm screwed. Thanks a lot Joe." Not able to bear any more statistics or facts, I slammed the lid of my computer down.

"Not me, I handle stress well. About as resilient as they come." Feeling a well of anger rise within, I was enraged my normalcy was taken away from me without warning.

All the articles stated "survivors" should get professional help to move through the trauma as soon as possible.

I went shopping.

Then I went to happy hour.

Not that I have anything against therapy. I'm all for it. I spent several years sitting in a therapist's chair around the time of my first divorce, but the thought of having to "talk" and bring to life what I was feeling right then felt impossible.

Retail therapy feels better than talking to some shrink, I thought. I was in the mall holding up a large sparkly necklace up against my chest, admiring it in a small mirror next to the cash register as I plucked down my credit card.

And that sexy dress on the dummy will certainly make me feel better. I talked my way through the mall with a sense of entitlement I'd never experienced before. It was as if I was owed something for having to go down this horrific path that I did not choose.

By trying to feel some sense of control in my life, I started to act even more out of whack. Something in me knew this effort to fill in the black hole of grief wasn't exactly rational nor was it the healthiest way to grieve, but I didn't give a damn. I did it anyway, and although I was clear it was just a *Band-Aid*, the brief moments of feeling "normal" and "in control" were worth it to me at the time.

After several shopping splurges, unbeknownst to my husband I charged up two credit cards he did not even know existed. Wanting nothing more than to fill the gapping void I felt, I used my funds and took out a loan for several personal development workshops and to build my coaching website that I knew James would not approve me spending money on. We managed our finances very differently from day one and my grief just exasperated the gap. I was all about expanding and healing. He seemed to be satisfied with life being the same way day in and day out.

Being able to do these things my soul sensed it needed in order to heal felt like a matter of life or death for me. I earned a good living and having to ask for permission to do the things I felt I needed to heal made me feel controlled and very angry. Yet I couldn't find the courage to address it. I knew he would just shut me down, so I pushed my feelings away.

At first splurging on clothes, decadent dinners, nice wine, and any workshop I could attend made me feel like I was celebrating life, moving forward, pumping money into the economy, and living for the moment. Soon I realized, I was attempting to source my power from outside myself and numbing my pain. I knew it was impossible to succeed going this route, but I was like a runaway train that couldn't be stopped. What I did not realize, was I was in the midst of a complete breakdown. Smack dab in the middle of my wrecking ball experience, yet blind to what was truly happening.

My energy reserves low, I found myself saying, "You deserve to take the day off from the gym," as I would sit in my living room in my workout clothes, thinking about what I was going to eat for dinner that night, instead of lacing up my sneakers.

Going back to work at my corporate job and continuing on as a coach for the 90-day Leadership program I was participating in helped me resist focusing on Joe 24/7, but the energy of the tragedy seemed to follow me wherever I went. I would walk into a business meeting and everyone would ask, *"How are you?"* with looks of concern and pity. Their pinched faces made my stomach turn.

My intense grief over Joe's suicide had the potential to make those around me feel uncomfortable and I wanted to avoid creating a scenario that made other people wince, so I gave them the answer I'd thought they were looking for: "I'm doing well, healing, and feeling better every day. Thanks."

As the weeks passed by, my "I'm doing great" line felt more and more false, but I kept at it while praying that something would shift for me. As each month wore on, I found all this lying made it harder to get up in the morning.

Focus on the distinctions you are teaching in your coaching program, my inner voice would silently whisper to me as the abyss I was engulfed in seemed to grow wider and deeper. *You get to interpret your circumstances. Empower yourself. You are not a victim,* my inner coach would continue doing its best to snap me out of my tailspin.

Yeah, Yeah, Yeah, whatever...I still feel shitty, I'd think as I strained to do something productive. Although the people I was coaching were getting amazing results, I was struggling to apply the same principles I was teaching them to myself. *I'm all fucked up, but at least I'm helping other people heal,* I'd reason with myself when the participants would share their excitement with me about what they were creating during the program.

Vacuuming my house felt like running a marathon. Doing the dishes was overwhelming. I hovered over my kitchen sink, feeling like a zombie in an infinite trance. Lifting my arms and picking up the sponge felt virtually impossible. *Maybe if I stand here and stare at this pile of dishes long enough, they will just wash themselves.*

What's going on here? Isn't all grief alike? I questioned myself. *This feels very different from losing Mom and Gram. Maybe I'm not a true grief expert after all.*

During my research I discovered there is something called complicated grief, which is a prolonged reaction to grief that is common for suicide survivors. *Yeah, maybe that's it,* I thought trying to convince myself I was normal and wasn't losing my mind. Then there was always the possibility I was in full PTSD (post-traumatic stress disorder) mode which is also common for people who lose someone in this manner. Neither of these possibilities seemed very appealing to me. *Perhaps Elizabeth Kübler Ross forgot to add a sixth stage to grief...CRAZY!*

Soon I didn't even bother to put my workout clothes on anymore and stopped going to the gym altogether. Within 3 months I gained fifteen pounds, which turned into another reason to continue my shopping sprees because now I couldn't fit into my pants. Any sense of self confidence plummeted.

Pretending to function wasn't only for myself. I didn't want my boss to think I wasn't up to my responsibilities or the people I was coaching to think I lost my edge and my ability to successfully coach them. Nor could I bear the thought of my friends not calling me or my husband and family being dragged down by my grief. This technique of self-management had me circling a drain of despair.

And while my husband was very supportive at the time of Joe's death, it became very apparent within a couple of months that he had very little patience for my grieving process. One afternoon I was explaining to him how upside down my life felt since Joe's death. "You need to get over it," James said.

"You don't get over your brother hanging himself from the attic rafters in the bedroom you grew up in." Deep resentment started to rise within me. "You've never lost anyone James this close to you. Both of your parents are alive and all your siblings."

"Well, I know how I would react if I did, and I would just move on." Not making eye contact with me, James shuffled the mail around on the kitchen counter.

"Easy for you to say." I left the room to go sit outside under my tree feeling completely misunderstood.

He wanted the old Kerry back. And not only could I not produce her for him, on a deeper level I knew I would never *be* her ever again. Being in the center of grief can be very lonely.

"Will I ever feel whole again?" I whispered to the "Healing Tree" after my argument with James. I began to wonder anxiously as I watched the leaves on the tree bend with the wind, "Am I even *capable* of moving through this?"

Making believe that I was okay was creating more and more space between me and other people. As the weeks passed, I went deeper and deeper into my blue cocoon, but made sure my hair was done and my lip gloss was applied seamlessly as to not alert anyone that I was drowning in darkness.

I began to feel ashamed that I was pursuing outside pleasures to dull my grief, trying to gain a sense of equilibrium. Judging myself on how poorly I was grieving, I would say thing like "You suck at this," as I sat on the couch not wanting to move a muscle. "You are not a depressed kind of person. What's happening to you?" I would ask myself as I stared in the mirror, while fear of what was becoming of me snaked through my being.

Putting pressure on myself, I acted as though I was going to get a grade when it was all over. As though there was some test I had to pass, but I wouldn't without cheating.

The one thing I was looking forward to during this very dark time was that James and I had a trip planned to Aruba with his cousin George and wife Megan. They had come over two weeks before Joe died for a family barbeque to celebrate James's birthday.

"We bought a time share in Aruba," George happily announced. We were sitting in our backyard finishing dinner. "Would you like to join us this fall for a week as a kind of birthday gift?"

George barely finished his sentence when I enthusiastically replied, "Absolutely! Yes!" James had a deer in headlight kind of a look. He wasn't sure what I was signing us up for.

"Yes?" James said with a look of disbelief. Clearly, he was afraid this was going to cost him a million dollars. "YES!" I said. "We are going!"

We hadn't traveled without our collective children for more than two years and I knew it would be fun to vacation with George and Megan. I had been to Aruba twice before and loved it. George, being the family planner, had the week booked by the end of the night. With the fun energy and unused frequent flyer miles on my side, James agreed to the trip.

After Joe's death, just imagining myself on a beach in the Caribbean gave me something to be excited about, perhaps *this* would be my first real opening to heal.

The beach had always been my happy place. Gram introduced me to the ocean as a young girl. We would walk on the sand along the water for hours collecting beach glass and soak up the healing vibes.

The beach is where I first really got a true sense that I was more than just a body bopping around life aimlessly, but I was a soul IN a body *with a purpose to fulfill* during my time here on earth. Feeling connected to universal life force energy automatically happens the moment I set my eyes on any body of water. *Surely feeling the spirit within me will bring me comfort and healing,* I thought. Visualizing myself gazing at the turquoise Caribbean Sea, smelling the salt air, and swishing my feet around in the fine white sand, I could feel myself let go just a speck.

Finally, I had a positive and grounding force. Perhaps I would find my way back to myself on that tiny little island.

~Chapter 5~

Fumbling for Meaning

"Every t-shirt, sun dress and pair of shorts I throw in my suitcase, brings me one step closer to high tailing it the hell out of here." I was deep into a power packing session for Aruba.

"I feel like I am going backwards instead of forwards most of the time," I whispered. Meticulously, I lined up my shoes in front of my suitcase.

Even though I had chosen to live more authentically and passionately in my life, to look for the gifts in the painful experience, that awakening still hadn't happened for me. Not even close. I'm so grateful I didn't know at the time. I was still a few years away from the layers being completely pealed back. Who knew awareness around my deep sense of unworthiness would ultimately lead to healing so much more than my grief?

"I *really* wish I could go meditate on a mountain somewhere for a few months and contemplate the meaning of life, but since that isn't an option, a week in the Caribbean will have to do." Sorting through my selection of strappy sandals, I decided I was grateful to just be getting away.

After a couple of hours of packing I headed to my favorite salon to get rid of my mixture of dark brown and gray roots that I had been too distressed to take care of. As I sat there with what felt like ten tons of foil on my head, Nick who cuts my hair came over.

"How are you doing?" Nick asked in the warm friendly upbeat tone he always uses to greet me.

"Much better, almost back to normal." I nervously adjusted myself in my seat, smoothing out the dowdy brown smock I was wearing to protect my clothing from the hair dye.

Without a warning my inner voice scolded me. *You liar.*

Okay, fine. Be that way. I restated my status to Nick, "Well, I intend to be back to normal come 10 days from now, when I return from my trip to Aruba." I gave him a big forced smile, teeth and all.

Most people swallow my *"much better and almost back to normal"* syrup and just move on with their version of a normal conversation not wanting to confront the depths of what I was dealing with.

Not Nick.

He surprised me with his answer. "You are *NOT* back to normal, what the hell is that, *normal?*" Standing behind me, his hands pressed against my upper arms as we both peered into the mirror, our reflections staring back at us. "How could you be? You are finding a *NEW* normal. Things will never be the same for you."

Feeling a shift in my being, it was if someone just put smelling salts under my nose.

I was ready to hear what he had to offer. Suddenly feeling a huge sense of relief, I realized as I sat in that chair becoming blonder by the moment that the goal was not to "be back to normal" but to "find my new normal," a new way of being in this world that no longer included my brother.

That simple shift in thinking made me feel immediately lighter, hopeful even. "Thanks Nick." I continued to look at our reflections in the mirror, fiddling with a foil that fell in front of my eyes. "Yes, you are *so* right on. I needed to hear that. My new normal is what I am committed to creating." Smiling, I realized this meant embarking on a completely different journey, than I had been trying to take to no avail. This new way felt better.

When I got back home and continued with my packing, I ran across a pile of pictures of Joe that I had used in the collages I had put together for his wake. This huge wave of anger rushed over me as I stuffed the pictures into a kitchen drawer. "Let's find out if out of sight, equals out of mind." I slammed the drawer shut and poured myself a big glass of lemon water.

At first, I felt myself trying to not feel the emotions rising within me, as I took out my trusty paper towels and cleanser, wiping down the counter tops frantically. Then without any thought I raced back over to the drawer, took the pictures out, and smashed them down on the counter.

Several of the pictures fell to the floor in a heap. "Screw this. I need to get this out!"

I looked at one of Joe's pictures and continued, "I'm pissed off at you Joseph for killing yourself and leaving the rest of us here to deal with your absence and how it is affecting all our lives. *How dare you?"* Sweat started beaming up on my forehead.

"Do you have any frigging idea the hell I am going through because you decided you didn't want to live anymore?"

As my eyes filled with tears, I grounded myself in my breath, and repeated the mantra that had been holding me together since I got the "Joe hung himself" phone call from Kim.

Breathe in, breathe out, I repeated several times to myself as I glared at Joe's pictures feeling ready to go at it with him.

"I didn't want to be mad at a drug addict *crazy* person!"

Feeling the anger as I stood there reflecting on the past few months, all the pain I had been experiencing and trying so desperately to suppress came bubbling up.

Rolling up my sleeves, it was as if I was about to climb into a boxing ring with my opponent. "The gloves are coming off, bro." Choosing one 6 x 4 black and white picture out of the pile, I brought it into the living room with me.

The picture was a close up of Joe's handsome, yet serious looking face. As I stared into his big brown eyes, I felt as though he were looking right back at me. The picture was eerily life like, as if at any moment I may see his eyes blink or he may suddenly flash a smile back at me from the photo.

Propping the picture up on a pillow, I began, "Ok, brother. Let's have a little chat. I have a few things that I need to get off my chest. This setting will have to do, since you went and took yourself out."

I kept staring into his eyes as I gazed at the picture imagining we were sitting knee to knee, so close we were touching. There was no room to run or hide.

"Didn't you think about us? Did you ever consider the aftermath of your actions and how broken it would leave us all feeling?"

The picture slipped down the pillow, falling face down on the carpet. Picking it back up, I repositioned it. "How desperately sad and confused we would all be? How dare you do this Joe? How dare you?"

Clearing my throat, I continued. "What about me and Kim? You know, *she* found you and gets to live with that image for the rest of her life! You didn't even *mention* us in the notes you left. No goodbye. No, I love you. No, it's been nice knowing you. NOTHING!"

The words and the emotions flowed through my lips and my being. I continued to lock eyes with Joe feeling his heart and his spirit tell me, *"I didn't mean to hurt you all."*

It wasn't about us at all in fact. Just then, I remembered something I read during my research that said suicide is not about ending life, *it's about ending pain.*

It was his own pain that moved him to do what he did, and considering anyone else's feelings wasn't even an option for him at the time, I thought while bringing his picture close to my face.

"I love you Joe. I miss you so much. I am so sorry that you were in so much pain and there was nothing I could do to help." I continued talking to the black and white photograph. "I wish I understood the depths of your mental illness and how to help you. The drug use tainted my vision. I'm so sorry."

As I sat there conversing with the picture, I imagined Joe's and my own spirit communing. Still envisioning us sitting knee to knee, I closed my eyes.

There was so much inherent goodness in Joe's soul, although it would get buried at times when he went to his dark place. Those of us closest to him would almost get amnesia about how beautiful he truly was on the inside when his crazy switch got turned on. Sitting there on my couch, I didn't want to think about his dark side. *Let me focus on the light*, I thought feeling my heart grow heavy. Contemplating why I loved him so made the hole he left feel bigger.

One Christmas not too long ago, he didn't have any money so he hand knit matching scarves for the entire family. Giving them to us on Christmas Eve, we all tossed them around our necks, looking like a misfit version of the Von Trapp family with our matching attire. "You look marvelous!" he proclaimed.

Joe whipped out his camera and started taking pictures of us. I could feel him oozing pride from finding a way to gift us with something from his heart that would be unforgettable.

So Mom could feel the energy of the place that she loved the most in the world during her final days on earth, Joe went over to our summer house in Kismet, Fire Island and brought back sand and beach grass from in front of our home. Creating unique sculptures was one of his hobbies, so he made a gorgeous arrangement of the beach grass and sand in a beautiful bowl and put it at Mom's feet as she lay dying in our family den.

He handed out little bags of Kismet sand with Pink Ribbons tied around them to everyone that attended her funeral. In my own swirl of grief, my legs felt like they weighed two tons as I walked away from Mom's casket at her gravesite. Struck by the courage Joe possessed to stay until her coffin was lowered into the ground, I watched from my car window as he poured sand from Kismet down into her grave. The love he had for our mother was palpable, as I watched him doing his best at 23-years-old to send her off with as much peace and adoration as possible.

Flashes of many more images of our lives together flooded my mind. From opening presents on Christmas morning when we were kids, to coming home to find Joe playing bongo drums on our front lawn. He was singing Latin songs at the top of his lungs so all the neighbors could hear. Then there was the unique event of watching him toss fire over at the beach to entertain anyone who wanted to watch the one man show he created. I thought about his incredible dance moves and the belly laughs we would share over the silliest things.

Never again will I have someone call me up on my birthday to sing me a compilation of Happy Birthday in Spanish and Today is Your Birthday by the Beatles, I thought realizing how much I looked forward to his call every year. The tears started flowing even quicker from my eyes as I imagined what my first birthday without him would be like.

Like Mom and Gram, Joe was a person I felt completely safe being myself with. Even when he was in his darkness, he provided a space for me to feel deeply loved for the totality of who I am, messy parts and all. Choking on my tears, I wondered how I would be able to live in a world without the love of these three treasures in my life.

Wanting the heavy darkness out of my body, I took a few more deep breaths. On my last exhale, I intentionally breathed out forcefully any last remnants of anger and let them dissolve into the air.

When we landed in Aruba, I felt like I touched Holy Ground. The minute my toes hit the sand, it was as if some unseen force was going to suck all my sorrow and anxiety right out of my body. I had an appointment with the universe. I was checking my bags in, ready to find my new normal.

Years ago, I read a piece on the internet by Carolyn Myss about, "calling your spirit back." According to Myss, "In every stored memory and instance of holding onto life's hurts and injustices we leave a little piece of our spirit energy there too – keeping hold of that pain. Add up those instances we all encounter over the average lifetime and you can imagine just how much energy is taken in storing those painful thoughts and memories. This is energy that is taken from the spirit within us now, wanting to live life and embrace the world we have here."

I knew I was here in Aruba to call back my spirit and reclaim the parts of me that I felt had disappeared over the past several months and perhaps even way before.

Grateful for some alone time, I made my way to the beach. I walked slowly and intentionally towards the crystal-clear water. The sky was a deep azure blue painted with long sweeps of pink that Grandma used to call a "sailor's delight." It was breathtaking and worthy of pulling up a chair as so many people were doing to witness the daily miracle of the sun going down.

Walking down the beach a bit more to give myself a little privacy, I whipped out my *iPhone* and snapped several pictures. Dipping my feet into the water, I was delightfully surprised with warm sensations filling my body.

I watched the sun lower itself into the water as I knelt in the sand. Then I closed my eyes for just a moment to ground myself in what I was about to say, as I didn't want to miss even one second of the beauty before me.

Pulling my hands together in a prayer position, I held them close to my heart while kneeling. The soft wind gently blew back my hair as I breathed in the peace filled air. "I am here to call my spirit back," I said quietly to the sea. "May all the powerful bits and pieces of me that have vanished since Joe's death come forth and be as one here in this body of mine." Speaking with as much authority and determination I could muster up. I wanted to make sure the universe knew I meant business.

"And so it is." I bowed my head in reverence and my heart filled up with gratitude as I knew for certain things were about to shift.

What will it be like to just let go? I wondered as I got myself ready for the beach the next morning. I couldn't even remember the last time I wasn't putting effort into holding myself together. James and the rest of the gang went to the supermarket to restock our groceries for our refrigerator in our suite, so I was on my own for the morning again.

Since the week I had taken off after Joe's death to just be still and fully take in what had happened, I felt like I had been moving at the speed of light despite the exhaustion, anxiety, and depression ganging up on me.

As the hotel elevator doors opened on the ground floor next to the pool, my heart began beating its way out of my chest. "Is this excitement or am I having heart palpitations?" I asked myself. Gently placing my hand on my chest, I could feel the pounding of my heart vibrating in my ears.

Stepping out of the elevator slowly, I felt faint. I was also experiencing this strange buzzing sensation in my head like I was trapped in one of those fly-zapping machines people keep in their backyards on hot summer nights. *This is not excitement,* I thought as I broke out in a cold sweat.

Trying not to draw attention to myself, I went and put my back up against the wall. *Breathe in, breath out,* I told myself over and over while doing my best not to black out. *Maybe I'm all spun up due to walking too fast,* I reasoned as I felt my heart begin to dial back down to a safer range. Even the buzzing sensation slowly disappeared.

When I finally made it to the beach, I looked down at my feet in the sand yet once again, rejoicing that I was back on Holy Ground.

Continuing my conversation with myself, I attempted to feel better about my recent little episode. *That was scary, but I'm sure it is nothing.* I had experienced that same strange sensation a few times over the season and was chalking it up to just being off balance from trying so hard to stay above water as I grieved.

Who wouldn't feel anxious after their brother is found hanging in their childhood bedroom? I wrote it off as a universal given that anxiety often includes light-headedness, heart palpitations, and a scary buzzing in the head.

A physical is definitely in order when I get home, I concluded as I made my way down towards the ocean finding an empty palapa to sit under in a prime beach area.

A 42-year-old woman shouldn't have to stop twice on a five-minute walk to the beach carrying only one light bag in her hand, right?

"Would you like towels Ma'am?" One of the bronzed twenty-something beach attendants approached me immediately as I set my bag down. "Yes, please." I pulled a well-worn empty lounge chair over to the spot I'd found.

Forgetting how intense the sun felt on the beach in Aruba, before I knew it, I had beads of perspiration on my forehead and chest. "Whew. Damn it is hot!" Watching at least 50 people swimming or floating in tubes in the ocean just a few yards in front of me, I decided it was time for a dip.

As I approached the edge of the water, I recalled how my mother always encouraged me to take a dip in the ocean when I had a cut on my toe or some other place. *The salt water heals wounds,* she would say. Surely enough it always seemed to work. My cut would be nearly gone the next day.

As I made my way further and further into the water leaving the shore behind, I had to navigate around the rocks that lined the first few feet of the ocean, to avoid cutting my feet open.

Inching my way to where the sand felt as smooth as silk beneath my feet, my hips were now level with the water. I couldn't help but wonder if it worked the same way with soul wounds.

Could this water speed up my healing? I breathed in the possibility and made the silent intention from my heart, *May I be healed,* as I submerged myself in the ocean.

Holding my nose tightly, I kept myself under as long as I could envisioning the trauma leaving my body. Then forcefully I stood up tasting the salt around my lips, as I brought my head back above water. *Time will tell if that worked.*

Making my way back to my chair, I dug through my bag for my journal and pen. *This trip will be over before you know it. Time to get busy girl,* I said to myself as I looked for a clean page to begin.

Although I had spent hours and hours lying on the beach, my nervous system still felt eerily on high alert. I was concerned that all this laying around hadn't banished the thread of fear I felt hovering inside my body.

"What's it going to take for me to let go and create a shift?" I wondered out loud. I placed my pen on the paper. "You said you were here in Aruba to call your spirit back."

Well? Is your mission accomplished?

My inner voice responded loud and clear, as I let out a big sigh. Obv*iously not, since you are still feeling like a train wreck.*

Continuing to inquire to some power within me, I hoped my pen would magically start writing to reveal what I was seeking. With all my heart I believed my inner voice held all the answers.

Brainstorming about what I was missing, I focused on solving why a feeling of fear seemed to be at the forefront of my daily experience. I scribbled down a few paragraphs about the trip and what I was discovering about myself. Then I turned to the next page and wrote down some more thoughts about what the past three months had been like since Joe left us behind.

Dig deeper. I heard my inner voice encouraging me as I continued to write. Wanting the Universe to swoop in and help me get unstuck, I looked out towards the sea in search of answers.

I can't go home without some sense of what I'm dealing with here. I cradled my journal like it was a dear friend intently listening to me. *I know I've been grieving, but I feel like some sort of switch inside me was turned that dreadful day and I can't seem to turn it back to where it was.*

Then I remembered the conversation I had with my hair stylist Nick about finding my new normal and reassured myself it wasn't about going back to who I was.

Who am I now? I continued to wonder as I tapped my pen in a steady rhythm on my note pad. *How am I going to grow and expand because this happened?* I demanded answers while scribbling passionately on the placid piece of white lined paper.

I know something is holding me back from stepping into the new life that I am now creating because this happened. What is it?

Then it fell upon me.

"Vulnerability," I whispered out towards the turquoise water.

I've been unwilling to be vulnerable and that is why I've been staying stuck. That is why I've been feeling so afraid. I've been in massive protective mode.

Vulnerability had never been my style. In fact, I was horribly allergic to the word. Sort of like someone who has a bad peanut allergy. I couldn't even be in the same space as what I deemed a weakness. It made me itch just thinking of it.

Awareness around my resistance to being vulnerable, would be the first layer of my healing and transforming my belief system around my value.

When I was 15 years old, I was held up at gunpoint with my best friend Jessica. Going against our parent's rules, we were out walking after dark getting ice cream. We were on Jessica's block when a man walked out of one of her neighbor's bushes with a gun pointed at us.

"Sit down on the curb," he instructed us. Locking arms, we sat. "Do you want money?" I asked as I offered him my spare change in my coat pocket.

As he was unbuckling his belt with his free hand it became clear he didn't want money. Within seconds one of Jessica's neighbors came out of their house to walk their German Shepard. The man with the gun peered over his shoulder eyeballing the neighbor and ran to his car.

Barely able to breathe, we burst into Jessica's house and within minutes her parents had the police at their home. My Mom and Vinnie arrived just after the cops. Mom was still in her bathrobe. Over the next couple of years, we would be brought down to the police station to participate in line-ups. It turns out that our perpetrator had sodomized several young women in our neighborhood.

Four years later I was reading the local newspaper, when I recognized the picture of a man arrested for a very similar crime. It turned out it was the man I had picked out at one of the line-ups we attended, but they were unable to arrest him back then, because not enough of the women picked out the same man.

Though not physically harmed by this incident, I thought I'd never feel safe again.

A year later I was raped at my family's summer home by someone I was dating. I was getting ready for work at the local burger shack, when he knocked on the door just as I got out of the shower. My family was on the mainland and I was alone. With a towel wrapped snugly around me, I reluctantly let him in. Instantaneously, he pinned me on a nearby day bed. He held my hands down by my side with such force I could not budge, as he used his legs to open mine and force himself upon me. I didn't tell a soul for years and completely blanked out the memory for over a decade.

But my nervous system remembered. From then on, I slept with a pair of sharp scissors wedged between my mattress and a baseball bat under my bed. Time, in my case, did not heal all wounds. Holding on to the terror gave me a fierce way to let everyone know, (including the universe), "Do not mess with me!"

I thought my innate softness put me at a disadvantage and I had even been made fun of for my tender heart when I was younger, so I shut that part of me down. Deciding that being soft and emotionally expressive made me like prey, I formulated a plan when I recreated myself after my divorce from my first husband. Little did I know leaning towards a masculine style of relating with other people and denying my innate femininity, would lead me further away from owning my worth as a woman.

My thick skin seemed to serve me well over the years, especially when I was rebuilding my life after my first marriage ended, or so I thought at the time. I saw my tenacity as a key component of my ability to excel in the corporate world.

What I didn't see was the emotional cost I would pay for the "mask" I was wearing. For years I pretended to be someone much tougher than how I felt inside, like I had it all together. Eventually, this uncomfortably thick skin became too tight and stressful.

Though I no longer slept with actual scissors or a baseball bat, I was still carrying them around with me metaphorically. My weapons though only imaginary, were still a powerful force in my life.

In 2011, I had taken a series of transformational workshops where I had received feedback about how people "experienced" me. According to the trainer, my "way of being" created a veil between other people and myself. My protective armor had me appear withdrawn at times, not fully present and unwilling to allow my authentic self to shine through. In retrospect, my coping mechanism of teleporting off into the unknown when things got stressful also played a big factor. How can you truly be with other people in such a way they will experience your soul, if you aren't even present in your body?

The weapons were also in place to hide my deep sense of unworthiness from the rest of the world. The veil was my way of making sure no one came too close and saw the real flawed me. Looking good to other people, not just physically, became a way of life for me. But all the glitzy chandelier earrings and professional accolades in the world could not cover up the energy I was exuding. People sniff out how we feel about ourselves. Energy never lies.

I put down the metaphoric scissors and baseball bat a bit before Joe's death realizing that living in such a defended way cost me the very things, I wanted to experience the most in life. Peace, love, joy and connection.

What I couldn't see before this moment on the beach was I unknowingly picked up my weapons and threw the veil back over my being the minute I received the phone call from Kim saying Joe ended his life.

Our cells in our bodies have memory, and in that precise moment of trauma finding out about Joe, mine got triggered and were put back on high alert. It felt as if all the healing I thought I had done through the years never even happened.

PART II

THE RECOLLECTION

The cave you fear to enter holds the treasure you seek.

-Joseph Campbell

~Chapter 6~

Mi Familia

Roast beef was always on Sunday. Mom made the most delicious meatballs every Tuesday and we had them for leftovers every Thursday. Just the smell of her homemade sauce put me into a delightful trance. Like Betty Crocker cooking was Mom's way of showing us we were cherished. Good food was one thing I could count on.

Meatball making was a sacred event in our home. Mom didn't have the recipe for the meatballs written down, so I learned how to make them the old-fashioned way. With my eyeballs. "Come here Kerry and watch me. This is how my Grandmother Carmella from Sicily taught me."

Wide-eyed I'd stand next to her, watching her grate fresh breadcrumbs from scratch. When it came time to put the parsley in, I would pay extra close attention since she used her hands instead of a measuring spoon. Occasionally, I'd get lucky and she would get specific. "One egg per pound of meat." If Mom was in a good mood, she'd even let me roll a few meatballs myself and place them gingerly in the frying pan.

Our attire often had us looking like we could be on the cover of a posh magazine. Even when money was tight, Mom made sure I got the Jordache designer jeans I desperately wanted for my ninth birthday. Kim's ribbons in her pig tails always matched her outfit perfectly. Joe often looked like he was going to work on Wall Street even though he was only a toddler.

Our home had often been full of laughter. Mom and Vinnie loved to make up their own song and dance routines to entertain us. It was fun having parents that were willing to be so kooky and made me treasure the magic of these lighthearted moments. Although I was adopted by Vinnie, he never made me feel like I was any different from his two biological children.

At times there was so much light and love in the home we grew up in, but there was also unimaginable angst that went along with being a member of my family.

The energy of our childhood home was one of duality. We never knew what we were going to get, particularly when it came to Mom. *This house is confusing,* I would think not understanding how one moment I could feel like I was in a loving safe environment and the next as though I lived smack dab in the middle of a war zone.

On a regular basis, I walked around the house with my pink rosary beads chanting the Hail Mary trying to ward off anything sinister. *Please God protect me. Make me feel safe,* I would pray over and over as I paced up and down the hallway outside my bedroom clutching my pretty beads. Imagining angels were watching over me, I hoped the fear I was feeling would one day vanish.

Soon after Joe was born in 1979, Mom stopped regularly showering and putting her make-up on for nearly two years. My once gorgeous blond bombshell mother started wearing the same clothes for days at a time. She was unrecognizable and barely left the house. When she did leave to drive me to school, I would hide in the back seat so none of my classmates would see me getting dropped off by her. The deep dark circles under her eyes screamed of incredible sadness and haunted my dreams as I attempted to accept this new version of my mother.

Soon the yelling would begin.

When sound levels would rise, I'd turn on both the TV *and* radio in my bedroom to drown out the noise and the threatening words. They were so loud the vibration of their voices made the walls seem like they were shaking. My walk-in closet became a nuclear like shelter for me when I hid within my clothes. My parents who barely said a curse word for years were suddenly dropping "F bombs" left and right.

My friends and our neighbors used to love to make fun of my parent's *loud way* of communicating as they would nicely put it. I'd do my best to chuckle along when someone would imitate my mother yelling, "VI-NNIE!" at the top of her lungs as if he was miles away, yet he was standing right next to her.

Oh my God she's crazy, I'd think as guilt washed through me for even thinking that thought. My inner critic would bark in my ear, *how could you say something like that about this woman who loves you so?* I truly believed it would be in my best interest to push all the nuttiness away, as if it was not happening and I was living in a functional environment.

You people have no idea what goes on in this house at night, I'd think as I'd break out in a sweat of shame. There didn't seem to be any other families I knew that were as consistently loud and utterly nasty as mine. *How could people that are supposed to love each other speak like this?* I was convinced that there was something seriously wrong with us and, quite possibly, God had me born into the "wrong" family.

Mom liked her Fleishman's rye whiskey and water every night, several of them. Once I heard the clinking of the first ice cubes of the evening hitting her glass, I'd cringe thinking, *time to strap yourself in!* Her loving light would quickly be overshadowed by her dark angry side.

I hope the fun-loving Mom hangs around at least for a little bit tonight, I would pray as I watched her fill her glass to the top. Soaking up every minute of when my mother was in a good mood, I'd chill out and chat with her in the kitchen as she cooked. Sitting there taking in the delicious aroma of whatever she was preparing that night, my heart would flood with love and gratitude for the gift of really being with my Mom in a soulful connected way. Knowing I was pretty much safe to converse with her up until drink number three, fear would eventually creep in. I knew for certain it was only a matter of time until she warped into the dark version of herself. After that, it was every man and kid for himself.

Joe was very similar to Mom with his mood swings, except he took it to a whole other level. Halo and horns all the way, it was if there were two people in his one body. He made Mom seem tame.

From the age of eighteen months, Joe would whip his plate like a Frisbee from his highchair, signaling to the rest of the family that he had finished his meal. By the time he was five, it would not be out of the ordinary for him to cut the tassels off Vinnie's expensive business shoes, redesigning them in such a way he could no longer wear them. He was also known to hang Vinnie's ties out on the white birch tree in the front yard and leave them flapping in the breeze if he didn't get his way.

Occasionally, Joe would bring Kim in on his act. One time they decided it would be fun to put a "For Sale" sign on Vinnie's car. Just like that, we had strangers knocking on our front door asking how much for the gold Cougar with deep bucket seats.

You never really had to wonder where you stood with Joe. He let you know.

"Joseph! You little son of a bitch," my mother shrieked one spring afternoon. "Knock that off RIGHT now!" Joe contorted his body as Mom tugged the back of his shirt trying to pull him from outside and back into our house to no avail.

He had thrown a large quantity of Vinnie's clothes (including his underwear) on the roof for no apparent reason. When Vinnie got home from work, he had to climb up a ladder to retrieve them. Slowly he climbed rung by rung to reach the highest peak of our home.

"Little bastard," Vinnie huffed under his breath.

Thank God, none of my girlfriends came over after school today, I thought to myself as I sat outside in a chair reading a book for English class, trying to not make eye contact with our neighbor that just pulled up in their driveway in time to witness Vinnie crawling on all fours across the shingles. Slumping down in my chair it felt l like I was being injected with a syringe of shame.

As Vinnie threw the clothes down, Joe kept throwing them back up from another angle as soon as they hit the lawn. "What is the matter with you? Stop torturing your father, Joseph!" Mom continued to plead with her unruly seven-year-old.

Joe flashed a look at her that warned, *"You are next on my hit list woman."* On a dime our mother switched her tone to sweetly let us know dinner was ready. Joe must have been hungry because he dropped the clothes in his hands and made his way into the house without further prodding.

Food always snapped my family back to some version of "normal." Vinnie was able to move all his clothes from the roof and into the house without being late for the first mouthful of steak, mashed potatoes, broccoli and carrots.

Granted, Joe's childhood wasn't the easiest. Besides living in our chaotic home, he was often mocked by other kids because he was "different" from the other boys. He loved dancing, singing, and everything Broadway. Kim regularly dressed him up as a girl, wig and all, which he didn't seem to mind. Joe graduated high school early to remove himself from all the angst and went away to college at age sixteen.

Then came his first Thanksgiving break.

He walked into our house with a fedora on his head (before they were back in style) and an electric pink fuzzy boa around his neck as my mother anxiously waited to greet him. "Joseph, my baby!" Mom gave him a big hug acting like she didn't notice his new attire.

This was a huge change in fashion choices since we dropped him off in August. Vinnie had a look on his face that said, "That was a long ride," as he hung his coat up in the closet.

What seventeen-year-old guy wears a boa and a fedora home from college? Instinctively, I felt something was up. Worried about mom and feeling protective over her health since she was going through chemotherapy at the time, my body tensed in anticipation of what was to come during this weekend visit. His energy felt erratic.

We went out to dinner that night as a family to the local Italian restaurant and Joe's behavior got weirder as the night went on.

"I'll have Penne a la vodka please." Joe ordered his dinner in a sultry voice that made my hair stand up. Then with a wink aimed at the waiter, he tossed his boa over his shoulder with a huge sweeping gesture and nearly hit the woman's head that was sitting behind him causing her to jump out of her seat.

A larger than life persona seemed to have engulfed his being as he continued to make big dramatic gestures with his hands for the duration of dinner, using the boa as a prop. When the boa landed in the breadbasket, I'd had *enough*.

"Put that fucking thing away if you know what's good for you!"

Joe stuffed the boa under his butt and turned away from me, pulling his Penne a la vodka close to his body.

"Well! Excuse me Missy!"

Wolfing down my chicken parmesan as I hunched down in my seat, I thought *Good God, I hope I don't run into anyone I know.* My parents sat there straight faced as though they didn't even notice Joe's behavior or new theatrical accessories. I couldn't decide if this comforted me or frightened me as I searched their expressionless faces while we ate dinner. Mom broke out in occasional giggles like a schoolgirl when Joe made a joke.

Maybe I am just having a crappy dream, I silently wished as Joe called a family meeting for "8 PM sharp" that evening as we left the restaurant. *Wasn't this enough together time?* I wondered as I climbed into my car wishing the night was over.

We all filed into the den (minus Kim) at "8 PM sharp" as instructed. Mom was going through chemo and had taken her wig off that made her look like *"Carol Brady"* according to the kids at the elementary school where she was the school nurse. She sat in her little pink beanie covering her bald head. Vinnie remained quiet. An apprehensive look was on his face.

Here it comes, I said to myself as Joe plopped himself down on the loveseat.

"I'm gay!" He tossed the boa over his neck again in a dramatic fashion, as though he were Liberace about to give a concert to a sold-out crowd.

No shit, I whispered to myself. I then quickly said, "Congratulations, I'm happy for you!" with as much glee as I could muster up after the dinner we just endured.

Instantly, Vinnie started crying and Mom looked baffled, as she whipped off her beanie exposing her bald head and started fanning herself with it.

I was truly happy for him that he was coming out at 17-years-old, though I wished he could have toned down all the theatrics and left the boa in his room. As I looked at my parents shell-shocked faces fumes of rage seemed to rise from my pores. *Thanks for coming home for a couple of days, dropping the bomb, and then leaving me to pick up the pieces.* But it was what it was. Truth is always better than the right time to tell it.

Later that night after decompressing, I plunked myself down next to Mom on the couch in the den. Her pink beanie was securely back on her head.

"Did you know Joe was gay?"

"I've known since he was three Kerry."

Within a couple of days, Vinnie dried his tears and life as we knew it went back to normal.

Of course, "normal" takes on a whole new meaning, when referencing my family. The following summer we were over at Fire Island and were sitting on the packed beach together. It was a rare event to have Mom and Vinnie make the quarter mile walk through town to sit by the Atlantic. Kim had her new boyfriend with her, and my son Matt was with us for the weekend also.

Out of nowhere Joe came sprinting onto the sand towards our beach chairs. His long sarong flowed behind him coming loose, revealing some odd version of a speedo. In addition to his beach bag, he was carrying a gigantic rainbow flag that could be seen for miles. "Mi Familia! So great to see you all," he greeted us. With that, he jammed the stick part of his flag into the sand like a beach umbrella, plopped himself in a chair, and took out a book to read.

"Look Mommy! It's the Jamaican flag." My seven-year-old son shouted as he bounced up from digging in the sand, pointing at the flag. "Yes, honey. How about that?" We hadn't told Matthew Joe was gay yet simply because it hadn't come up. My head quickly turned to look at my parents. Simultaneously, they shrugged their shoulders and grinned at me.

Yes, everything was certainly back to normal.

~Chapter 7~

Breakdowns and Breakthroughs

Danny and I started dating when I was twenty years old. Though he was three years older than I am, we had known each other since high school. He was a star varsity football player and I was a cheerleader for the freshmen team.

Our first date was a long drive out to Montauk Point, Long Island. We didn't have the intention of driving all the way out to the end of the island, but the talking between us flowed effortlessly and, before we knew it, we were parked outside of *Gurney's Spa and Restaurant*. Though a native Long Islander, I had never been there before and was excited to broaden my horizons.

"Want to go in for a bite?" Danny flashed a smile and opened his car door before I even had a chance to answer.

"Sure. I'd love to." My heart raced as he escorted me into the restaurant.

Gazing at the Atlantic Ocean from our window side table, I knew this date was different than any others I had been on. Dan was smart, handsome, and successful as an accountant. His sense of humor was endearing. I felt like I was with a real grownup.

Both of us liked to socialize and have the same kind of fun. He was from a large family that seemed much more functional than mine, so that was a plus. Most important, I respected his values.

Less than two months after that first date, I discovered I was pregnant with Matthew.

How did I go from being a young woman that was in the National Honor Society, editor of her high school yearbook, Varsity cheerleader, and a happy-go-lucky sorority girl in college; to now be a young unwed mother? As I contemplated the direction my life seemed to be taking, little zings of electricity bounced around my body as if I was being made aware big changes were about to take place for me. Staring at the positive pregnancy test, while simultaneously placing my hand on my belly, I realized I was now "that girl" people would be whispering about in the local supermarket. And they did.

After a night out with Danny to discuss our situation, I came home to find Mom stuffing artichokes for Christmas dinner which would be the next day. Sticking with my regular routine I had since I was a kid, I plopped myself in a chair while she was cooking to chat with her.

As Mom stared me down, she placed the artichoke she was stuffing on a platter.

"Are you pregnant?"

The tears streaming down my face answered her question.

She picked up the artichoke and continued to stuff it without missing a beat. After a few moments of dead silence as she worked her way through the stack of artichokes, she cleared her throat before starting to speak.

"Don't worry, everything is going to be okay."

Within days our immediate families knew that I was pregnant. Everyone had an opinion. While I am sure all the people involved had our best interest at heart, it was difficult to take in all the wide range of suggestions. Everyone seemed to know what was best for me, except me.

Wanting to give our baby the best possible beginning we could,

Danny and I decided to get married a couple of months later. Matthew was born five months after our wedding.

"Oh my God Danny, look how big he is!" Though I had been feeling Matt swim inside my belly for months, I was overcome with awe in the delivery room when I first laid eyes on his seven-pound twelve-ounce perfect body.

"I can't believe we made a real human being." I continued to express my realization and shock we were now parents. Fully responsible for this little soul being weighed and measured. The nurses handed our precious miracle over to Danny while the doctor continued to tend to me. Unable to take my eyes off Matt, I couldn't wait for the doctor to be finished with me so I could love him up.

We choose the name Matthew because it means, "Gift from God," and that was how we viewed his arrival. Within a couple of months his hair turned platinum blond and his eyes were as blue as the sky. Falling madly in love with this sweet little being, Matt and I spent 24 hours a day together those first couple of years. From day one, it was like our souls knew each other and we were meant to be mother and son.

Things were going so well with our marriage Danny and I decided to try to have another baby. I got pregnant again quite easily but experienced a series of miscarriages.

Danny had been very supportive with my first miscarriage. "Everything is going to be okay. We will try again," he reassured me. The second miscarriage, I fell into a depression. *I'm 22. I shouldn't have any problems having a baby,* I thought as I laid on the couch wondering what I should do next. I never imagined my body wouldn't function like it was supposed to.

As the weeks past, Danny grew impatient with my sadness. "It's time to move on Kerry." Although I knew he was right, I resented how quickly he was able to let go of the idea of having another baby.

Easy for you to say. You have a career. I can't even give Matt a brother or sister. And what kind of a future do I have with no degree?

One morning while watching Matt play outside, I decided. *Since the baby thing isn't working out, I guess I will reapply to college and finish my bachelor's.* Feeling proud of myself, I figured that type of forward thinking would be a great way to get myself excited about life again, and potentially alleviate some of the stress in my marriage.

"Oh boy, here it is!" The afternoon mail contained a letter from the local University I applied to. "It's Mommy's acceptance letter to go back and finish college!" Though he had no idea why I was jumping around, Matt grinned excitedly at me as he wolfed down his chicken nuggets and broccoli.

Except it wasn't an acceptance letter.

I'd been rejected.

Really? I thought to myself. *I'm rejected from a school that I easily could have gotten into after graduating from high school. How can this be?* I was stunned. I never even considered that I wouldn't get in.

Okay…plan A and plan B didn't work, so let me make a go at it with plan C. Picking myself up by my bootstraps, I decided that I would take a job and perused the Sunday classified ads looking for a position.

Having somewhere to go every day and bringing in a very few extra bucks perked me up a bit. Danny worked intense hours, many times coming home exhausted at 4 AM during his busy season just to get up early the next morning and do it all over again.

"You're never home and then on the weekends we are always with other people." Feeling depleted myself from working and taking care of a baby, I missed spending one on one time with Danny.

"I'm the breadwinner Kerry, I have to do what I have to do to provide for our family."

Who can argue with that? I thought. *I guess this is what it is. Welcome to adult life.*

Feeling disconnected, little by little the spark we shared continued to dwindle. The roles we assumed as parents and married people began to feel tight like suits tailored for other people. Except for the joy Matt brought me, a sense of emptiness haunted me daily. Not having the wisdom and relationship experience that comes with the benefit of age, I didn't even realize our marriage was gasping for air until it was too late.

As I continued to spiral down, losing my sense of hope or accomplishment as a couple, my sense of self also shrunk to nil. I didn't know who I was as an adult woman or where my life was going. In fact, I didn't even feel like a woman at all. I felt like a child trapped in an adult woman's life that I was not prepared to take on.

Within a month of this time, I met someone and had a very brief affair. Now I was miserable *and* guilty. Hating myself for being out of integrity with my husband and baby, I ended the affair and recommitted to making my marriage work.

Life as an adult was not what I expected. And what I suspected was that I sucked at it.

One afternoon at the height of my meltdown, I stood in front of the TV watching *The Oprah Winfrey Show,* as Matt pulled over some cushions and began to construct a fort around my legs.

Oprah's guest that day was author Marianne Williamson who was then discussing what would become her bestselling book *A Return to Love, Reflections on a Course in Miracles.*

Intrigued, I turned the volume up as Matt sat in his cushion fort eating his bowl of dry Cheerios. Marianne went on, "We can always choose to perceive things differently. We can focus on what's wrong in our life, or we can focus on what's right."

You mean I have a choice on what I focus on?

The idea of it seemed so radical to me, as if it came from another world or something. Up until this moment it felt like life was happening *to* me. I was focusing on everything that seemed to be going wrong for sure. This concept of choice changed everything. It was an invitation to view my life as if I had been given a new set of eyes.

Soaking up Marianne Williamson's words, my inner soulful compass kicked in: *All is not lost amid what is occurring. Perhaps there is a way out of the darkness. Loserville isn't my guaranteed destination just because my life took a turn into the unexpected and I've made mistakes. I can and will reinvent myself.*

That day is when my spiritual journey really began. And although I had a long-term relationship with the divine from the early days of cradling my pink rosary beads, there was an intense inner knowing this new voyage to the soul was different. Stocking up on as many books as possible over the next few months, I became a student of various metaphysical studies. *I feel so alive,* I would think whenever I drenched myself in these new concepts.

Something had to shift, and little by little, *I realized that it would have to be me.*

For years, I was unable to tie to together how the craziness of my family and the violence I was subjected to really affected the way I moved through the world. I realized it may be a good time to seek some therapy. By allowing myself to receive professional support, I was able share my past traumas in a safe place, putting the pieces of the puzzle of my life together.

Besides Mom and Joe's erratic behavior that always had my fragile nervous system on edge while growing up, the couple of other significant events that occurred in my teen years deeply implanted fear in my cells. Fear that would get activated after Joe's death.

I learned about cellular memory when I was voraciously studying spiritual concepts. The theory explains how our cells in our bodies store memories independent of our brains. Trauma can get stuck if we don't process or accept what has occurred. I read study after study on organ transplant patients, finding many wake up not with not just a new heart, but with preferences for things such as food or music their donor enjoyed while alive, all due to these inclinations being stored in cells.

Fascinated with the concept, I didn't know yet how cellular memory would play a huge part of me understanding the tremendous emotional pain I experienced after Joe's death. Eventually I would see I was not only dealing with the trauma of his suicide, but also all my unhealed trauma and wounds from my past.

When my best friend Jessica and I were held up at gunpoint it was the first time I felt on a visceral level that my life could be taken away from me at any moment. Though we were not physically harmed, I felt even more out of control about my ability to be protected. My already fractured nervous system went haywire.

A year later, when I was raped at our family's beach house on Fire Island, I never told a soul. I didn't even admit the truth of this offense to myself until I started therapy. Although I stuffed the memory down and inadvertently trapped it within my cells, looking back I realize I immediately started to sleep with my trusty baseball bat and scissors. I had always chalked up my nightly security routine to being held at gun point a year earlier.

These events helped solidify my belief system that *the world is not a safe place, better be on high alert all the time or you will get hurt. Emotionally and/or physically.*

With this new realization, boatloads of shame followed. Even though intellectually I realized that this violation wasn't my fault, the 16-year-old living inside of me felt guilty for even inviting him into the house that day. I already felt remorseful about being held up at gunpoint. One of my mother's rules was I wasn't allowed to be walking around at night in the neighborhood. She didn't hold back from reminding me, "if I had listened to her, it wouldn't have happened."

Dan and I continued to work on our marriage. We spent time together, ate dinner as a family, and worked on our house. Wanting to feel connected to him I shared what I was discovering about myself in therapy, including telling him that I was raped. Unable to find any words for several moments he leaned against the hallway wall and did his best to make eye contact.

"I am sorry that happened to you." We never spoke of it again.

One evening when he got home from work, I nervously read a passage from *A Return to Love* to him in our kitchen as I cooked dinner. "I accept the beauty within me as who I really am. I am not my weakness. I am not my anger. I am not my small mindedness. I am much, much more. And I am willing to be reminded of who I am." I read verbatim from the text. Looking up at him as I finished reading, I hoped to have a deep conversation on each specific passage shared, but he looked at me as if I were an alien and just laughed.

Starting to open my mouth to defend myself, I immediately stopped. I looked him directly in the eyes as he continued to smirk at me. Quietly, I walked back to the stove to stir the marinara sauce I was making for dinner.

"Never mind."

My internal voice piped in. *Not only is the world not safe, it is also risky to share your truths with others because you may be rejected. Laughed at even…*

Taking a breath, I took a moment to cast aside that old paradigm and aligned myself with the new beliefs I was developing from my spiritual studies. *Be yourself anyway,* I heard coming from a place inside of me that up to that moment I didn't even knew existed.

Just as I suspected, I was going to have to muster up a serious dose of courage to turn my life around. The woman who I'd dreamed about becoming when I was younger, was alive and well inside of me.

I just need to excavate her, I thought as I took a drive over to my mother's house the next day.

"Mom, I want to leave Danny. I'm miserable."

Pausing, I took a deep long breath. "And I did something really bad, too."

"What do you mean?"

The look on her face was a combination of concerned and annoyed. "What is going on with you?"

I went on to tell her how lost I'd been feeling, how miserable I'd become in my marriage. Then I laid it out there — the truth about my infidelity.

"I can't spend the rest of my life like this. I feel like I'm not living. I'm just existing; I have no idea who I really am." Tears welled up in my eyes as I gave a voice to my despair.

"Can Matt and I move in with you?"

Then the conversation took a turn in the complete opposite direction of my hopes when I'd played it out in my mind. Mom was completely non-judgmental around my affair (unexpected) but said a firm "No" to Matt and I living with her.

"What? Did you just say *no,* we can't live with you?"

"Yes, Kerry. You heard me correctly."

As I watched her wipe down the kitchen counter, scooping the crumbs from lunch into her hand and tossing them into the garbage, I felt like I was going to faint.

"Well, what am I supposed to do now?"

"I don't know, but you are not coming here."

Over the next few days, I thought about my options. I approached Dan, when I thought I had the answer.

"I want to separate. Could you leave the house so Matt and I can live here until we figure things out?" The knot in my stomach tightened as I squeezed out each word.

"I need to sit with all of this Kerry. Let's be sure to think things through."

"Ok, of course." I wanted everything to remain as amicable as possible between us.

A few days before this conversation, feeling like I needed someone to confide in, I had shared with my neighbor and friend Susan, that I had a very brief affair. She promised not to tell anyone. Unbeknownst to me she told her husband who then decided to tell Dan just a few days afterward.

Our home became an instant verbal war zone. "I will *never* leave this house and you will *never* take Matthew out of here. My family has money, and I can get the best lawyers." Dan was understandably seething.

"I will take you to court and prove you an unfit mother."

Somehow, we co-existed in that increasingly bleak house for nearly a month while I attempted to devise a plan. Dan's newfound temper did not simmer down, and the explosive environment grew more heated by the day.

My mother and my biological father had an unfriendly divorce. I didn't want my son to experience that kind of trauma and I wanted both of us to consistently be in his life. Contemplating my options, it did not seem like I had many of them. I would hear Danny's declaration repeatedly in my head, "I'm going to take you to court and prove you an unfit mother." I believed, for sure, that he would attempt to do this — the notion haunted me every night.

Taking out a pen and a sheet of paper during one of my sleepless evenings. I began scribbling:

Danny comes from a "normal" family, I come from a "crazy" family.
I'm the cheater and heathen and Danny is the innocent good guy.
Danny has a college degree, I don't.
He has a career, I don't.

His family has boatloads of money, mine doesn't.

As I reviewed my list, I felt so broken and began believing that maybe he was right. Maybe I was an unfit mother.

I had nowhere to go, no job, and no money. What I did have was a new will to live more honestly and a deep desire to create a life worth living. The spiritual journey I had begun over the past year infused me with courage. That would *need* to be enough for me to take at least one scary step forward.

A couple of days later, on instinct, I drove up to the North Shore of Long Island to a town called Huntington. Although it was only a half an hour away from where I lived on the South Shore of Long Island, I had never been there.

When I parked my car and walked around the quaint tree-lined town, with its brick buildings, boutiques and lovely restaurants, I felt a world away from where I'd come from. Loving the vibe of the place, I knew this would be the town where I would start over. Within a couple of hours, I found a job as a waitress and a small studio apartment.

I drove back to the South Shore straight over to my mom's. It was time to tell her my plan. "I'm leaving Danny even though you said I can't come here."

I went on to tell her how my "friend" told him about my affair and the ensuing madness that had been surrounding me in the days that followed. She looked horrified and a bit nervous as she began scratching her arm aggressively.

"He's going to take me to court to prove I'm an unfit mother and take custody away from me." I shared my worst fear that the entire world would find out how unsuited I was as a wife and mother and I wouldn't be able to see my Matthew.

"I don't have the money to fight him and I'm not quite sure I have the emotional strength right now, either. I asked him to leave the house and he said no, so I am going to leave. Somehow, some way, I'm going to get him to agree to joint legal custody."

"Can I stay with you for a few weeks while I save up enough money for an apartment I found?" I closed my eyes and held my breath for a moment, praying she would say yes this time. Deep down I knew that Mom's motivation in saying no to me moving in was to prevent me from getting divorced from Danny. From her warped viewpoint she was trying to spare me pain.

"Ok. You can stay for a few weeks. I'm not happy about this, but you seem intent on what you are doing." Feeling relieved, I gave her a big hug and then put both my hands firmly on her shoulders, looking directly into her blueberry colored eyes. "Thank you SO much. You have no idea how much this means to me."

When Danny walked in from work that night, I had already tucked Matt into bed. The living room was dim and quiet. Only one light was on and a small candle was burning. "I'm moving out tomorrow." Standing up from the couch, I slowly moved towards him. "I got a job and I'm going to stay with my mother for a little while until I can save money for a place of my own."

He looked stunned and, for the first time in a couple of weeks, couldn't speak.

"I'm requesting joint-legal custody. Matthew can stay here with you and I will take him with me a few times a week. We can work out the details over the next few days."

"I want to be the custodial parent or I'm taking you to court Kerry."

"Only if you agree to joint legal custody would I consider that Danny. The only reason I would even agree to it is that I don't want to put myself or Matt through a nasty custody battle."

Not saying another word, he walked right past me, went into the bedroom and closed the door. Sitting back down on the couch, I reached over some pillows and turned the light off. Only the glow from the single candle illuminated the room. It felt like a holy moment. Though not completely aware of the transformation that was starting to take place, there was a sense I was tapping into the authentic power I'd been searching for. The inner work I had been consistently doing made me brave enough to follow my intuition, even though no one else thought my choice was a very good idea. There was an inner *knowing* that we would *all* be okay.

It turned out the waitressing job I'd landed was not going to be enough to sustain a roof over my head. As a matter of fact, once I moved into my apartment, I needed to take a second job in an office. Working seven days a week to make ends meet and there was still a hell of a lot more days in the week than there was money in my pocket.

Matt and I ate a lot of macaroni and cheese back then. Thank God I was young and my metabolism was resilient. I shuttled Matt back and forth from my apartment to Danny's house several times a week in between my working hours.

It was exhausting and exhilarating all at once. Most of all it was peaceful.

Growing up in a house where screaming was the way people communicated and spending most of my marriage trying to contort myself into what I thought others wanted me to be, I had never experienced the immense peace I now felt. Silence allowed my true inner voice to emerge.

I was at the precipice of birthing something new.

Me.

Neon colored beach chairs were my furniture for a few months. Eventually Mom softened and surprised Matt and I with a new couch and entertainment center for our television. Scraping up enough money to buy a bookshelf, I placed it in my living room and treated it like an antique worth million's. My precious books became my best friends and filled my heart with hope for a better life that still seemed very far away for me. Mom deemed me the "Self-Help Queen" though I'm not quite sure she meant this title as a compliment.

Knowing there was a powerful woman inside of me that was just dying to get out, I didn't know how to unlock her cage and set her free. Though I was making some progress, I held myself small, focusing mostly on my shortcomings. I was unable to see my natural gifts.

Doing my best to release myself from my past, not long after Danny and I divorced, I decided to reveal to Mom I was raped.

She looks like she's in a pretty open mood. The dark switch hasn't been turned on yet, I thought as I approached the table where she was playing solitaire in the very same beach house where the incident occurred. *Okay, deep breath girl. Just say lay it out on the table.*

"Mom, when I was 16-years-old, I was raped, right here in this house." I gave as few details as necessary to not freak her out. Looking over to the space in the room where he held me down by my arms, separating my legs with his knees, I felt the weight of helplessness I experienced that day fall upon my heart.

Expecting her to gasp with sadness and shock, I hoped to hear, "Oh my God, my sweet daughter, I can't believe you went through that. Thank you for being brave enough to share it with me."

Instead I got, "Well you shouldn't have invited him over to the house when no one was home. It's your own fault."

Bada Bing. There you have it. Once again, guilty as charged.

Mom's curt response was followed by dead silence as she looked away and began reshuffling her deck of cards so feverishly, I'm surprised she didn't start a fire. Her choice to completely disconnect from me and my truth I was sharing made me feel invisible. In an instant, my worthiness meter went down yet another notch.

Not only is the world not secure, but you aren't safe to be yourself either. You may be rejected. Perhaps you aren't even worthy of acceptance if the closest person in the world to you shut you down like that.

I stood there stunned feeling myself shrink before her.

Immediately the light within me went out. Up went my armor and once again I made like it never happened, keeping my now metaphoric weapons firmly in place.

Guilt of my affair also haunted me for years. Like a ball and chain, I carried the weight of it with me wherever I went. Just when I would seem to move on from it, I would get a huge reminder every time I had to look Danny in the eyes when I would drop Matt back off. *You don't deserve to be happy after what you did,* I would hear in my head over and over, despite my valiant efforts to chuck that belief.

My heart yearned for Matt when he was not with me, but I never felt like I made the wrong choice. Danny started dating a woman Caroline a few months after we separated. They married a couple of years later and had two more children. They were able to give him all the things I couldn't. Stability, a big house, siblings, even a lovable and loyal yellow lab that Matt adored were all a part of my son's life, rightfully so.

Our custody arrangement gave me first class training in putting my ego to the side. I was not naïve to the fact that most people think if a child is not living full-time with their mother that there must be something "wrong" with her.

Enduring plenty of weird looks and awkward questions throughout the years, I did my best to not to let it chip away at my already fragile sense of self. *No, I'm not a crack addict or a nut job,* I'd want to say when people would get nosey. *Just a Mom who wanted the best for her child and was willing to admit that being full-time with me wasn't going to set him up for the greatest success in life. Go ahead judge me for it...*

Not seeing my biological father for many years and being adopted by Vinnie also had a profound effect on me. I clearly remember the day Vinnie, Mom, and I went to court to make the adoption official. I got a new last name and everything, which was kind of exciting as a 7-year-old. We went out to lunch to celebrate and I told every random stranger that happened to pass, "I just got adopted" as if I never had a parent a day in my life up to that point. My mother made me feel the adoption was a great idea and I certainly didn't want to disagree with her, so I went along with the process very willingly.

It wouldn't be until I was a parent myself that the scars started to emerge. I asked my mother if I could see my father when I was fourteen. We did start a relationship, but it always felt distant, like we were both scared of each other. As the years went on, I understood my mom did not make it easy for my father to see me when I was a young girl. She wanted things her way and apparently him out of the way. But the reality was that he choose to sign the paperwork to let me go. With perspective, I guess the young girl inside me could just never understand how my father could walk away from me potentially forever.

We all have internal narratives we make up about our childhood that shape the way we relate with ourselves and others as adults. The story I was living out loud was *I'm not worthy of love and sticking around for.* The energy I exuded was as though I had "not good enough" stamped on my forehead. *If my own father doesn't find me worthy of fighting for, how can I expect another man to?* My cells ached with the heaviness and hurt of it all, yet I had no idea how to climb out of it. Sensing there was nothing unique or special about me that would cause a man to stay, I created that scenario in every romantic relationship I entered.

It wasn't that I couldn't find anyone to date. I became quite adept at using my sex appeal and physical beauty to lure men in. Problem was that since I didn't love myself fully, I made it all about what I looked like and not who I was inside. I subconsciously set myself up to be treated like an object and not a human being with beautiful soul. I recreated my abandonment issues over and over again.

Forgiving others was the easier part for me. Forgiving myself was where I remained stuck. I wanted to be a mother that inspired and made Matt proud, despite my fears and mistakes. *One day I'll get there,* I thought as I gazed at my blond little boy, encouraging myself to keep trudging forward even when I felt completely lost.

When my health insurance ran out two years after my divorce, I decided to venture out into the corporate world so I would be covered medically. Perusing the Help-Wanted ads in my local newspaper, I saw an advertisement for a customer service representative at an electronics distributor. "Hmm, I think electronics is heading somewhere. This may be a good place to get my foot in the door." It was 1996 and I was 27 years old.

I went for an interview the next day. "You're hired," the manager declared at the end of my interview. Deep within my cells I felt a promising pulse this could be the start of something great for me. The pay wasn't much, but I was going to get the medical coverage I was seeking. I continued to work evenings and weekends as a waitress and for the first time in my life I was standing on my own two feet emotionally and financially.

My career blossomed year after year. As I gained new skills, I moved to a couple of different companies within the industry, eventually moving out of the administrative function and into more lucrative sales positions, and eventually management.

Gradually my outside world started to shift. I had been driving a beat-up Chevy with no heat or air conditioning. The gaping holes on the floor on the driver's side were big enough for me to see the pavement when I looked down. The car died at nearly every red light, so I kept jumper cables in my backseat just in case. Driving down the block to the store became an adventure. I became an expert at gliding towards the light, doing my best to avoid breaking to keep the car running. Within a few years I upgraded to a BMW.

I moved out of my original studio apartment, which would eventually become a magnet for all sorts of creatures. Situated on top of a restaurant, it wouldn't be unusual to find a dead mouse underneath a piece of furniture. The skylight had a hole where wasps would enter once the weather warmed up. Pretending a coat hanger was a bow and arrow, Matt would arm himself to protect me from the stinging creatures. "Stay away from my mommy you wasps!" he would command. Adorable as his gesture was, I felt horrible I had to bring him into such a crappy environment and was happy to move into a much more suitable space once I started to make more money.

Despite these life upgrades a sense worthiness still eluded me. I felt like an imposter.

~Chapter 8~

And When One of Us Is Gone

Mom started having back pain at the end of June 2002. The family doctor told her she had herniated disks. She started to go to physical therapy, but the pain continued to increase, until it became so excruciating that I showed up at the doctor's office in my pajamas one morning begging for a prescription of pain medication for her.

The doctor gave me the meds which proved to be a temporary fix. A couple of days later, Mom even managed to get up out of the chair in the den she was spending most of her time in and cook chicken cordon blue.

Sitting in a chair at the kitchen table like I had always done since I was a kid, we chatted as I watched her turn the cutlets. There was something different about this time though. I could not take my eyes off her, not even for a second. As if something deep inside me knew I wanted to etch this memory forever in my mind. Watching my mother do what she loved most for the last time. Cook a meal for her family.

"I think I did this to my back a few weeks ago when I was hanging curtains," Mom said as she placed the ham and swiss cheese on the chicken. Intuitively, I knew the pain was likely the breast cancer that had been in remission for six years coming back to haunt us for the last time and I was certain so did she.

We all boarded a ferry for Fire Island one morning in Mid-August for an annual Breast Cancer fundraiser that we always attended as a family, minus Joe. I could see it in Mom's eyes she knew what was happening as she winced in pain. Remaining mostly in our family cabana for the day, she visited with a couple of friends, but was clearly deteriorating quickly. Thirteen days later she would be gone.

As I gripped Mom's arm and gently helped her lay down on the bed, she looked at me squarely. "I hate looking in your eyes and seeing you look at me like you are looking at me for the last time."

Not realizing my face was expressing my inner most fears, I had no words. Kissing her on the head, I walked out of the room and back to the fundraiser not wanting to even connect with the truth of what she just said.

Joe and Mom were not on speaking terms at the time. He was deep "in his crazy" as he liked to call it. It appeared Mom couldn't bear him to reveal any more intimate details of his life to her, since all the love she gave him couldn't seem to stop him from destroying himself. His latest revelation to her was that he was selling his body sexually for drug money.

"He's what?" Stunned at this news, I plopped on the floor and leaned against the chair in the den Mom spent most of her last six weeks alive sitting in. I've seen and heard Joe do some wild things, but this felt unbearable. Surreal. As if it were a plot in a movie and not my brother's life. *How could this be? How did we get here?*

Joe started using drugs and drinking hard as a teenager. One day when we were having a heart to heart, he decided to tell me how his addictions began.

"I was nine when I started drinking."

"Nine!!!" Who starts drinking at nine besides Drew Barrymore?" Joking, I tried to brush off the sadness I felt from his disclosure.

We wouldn't realize how bad his problem was until he was in his early twenties. Crystal Meth was his "drug of choice." He used it on and off for over a decade until his death.

A week after our ferry trip to the beach we finally went to Mom's oncologist. After they took her blood, Dr. Silver pulled me out of the room.

"We are looking at a few weeks at best, Kerry. It's in her bone marrow. She needs to go to the hospital for a transfusion. Her platelets are low. She could bleed out."

Leaning against the wall in the hall to hold myself up, it felt like all my blood was being drained from my body. *Please God, don't let this be happening.*

"Then what?"

"Hospice." Dr. Silver scribbled some notes on Mom's chart and walked back into the examination room to give the rest of the family the news.

Dr. Silver's office was on the corner of Grandma Philly's block. Vinnie and Kim took Mom straight to the hospital and I jumped in the car immediately after the doctor gave us the prognosis and headed to Grammy's.

My mother and grandmother were also not speaking when we found out my mother's cancer was terminal. They cherished each other, yet their relationship like my mother's moods went in unpredictable cycles. It would be smooth sailing for years, then with one remark from my grandmother, Mom would decide they were never related in the first place.

Swiftly entering the front door without knocking, I cut right to the chase. "Mommy's dying."

Gram had become quite frail herself and was sitting in "her" chair in her living room, like I had seen her countless times before. For some reason she looked even tinier than usual as I blurted out the news.

"What the fuck do you want me to do about it?" Uncle John responded as he quickly stood up from the kitchen table. Mom and her brother John had been on the outs since Gram made a declaration, she was going to leave the house they grew up in only to him, which now seemed ironic since my mother was going to die first.

"Fuck you!" I desperately wanted to lunge at him. "Don't even bother coming to her funeral you asshole!"

"Grammy, I'm serious. The doctor says she has weeks. Please come! Your Patty girl needs you." Placing my hands on her lap, I knelt beside her. Looking up, I saw Gram was weeping.

My next call would be to Joe.

"Joseph. Mommy's dying."

"Like when?" His signature smart ass undertone was firmly intact.

"Like NOW jackass. Get home."

Joe showed up the next day and added dramatic flair to Mom's death like only he could do. "Who is that?" Dr. Silver asked me when Joe sauntered down the hospital hallway to Mom's room like he was on a catwalk at fashion week.

"Oh, that's my brother. He's on drugs. Don't pay any attention to what he says to you."

Apparently, Joe had been telling Dr. Silver he needed to give Mom chemo, which she was vehemently against going through again. Once we got her home, he did make an amazing Florence Nightingale. Administering Mom all the meds she was on, I became quite suspicious he was slipping himself a few of her pills as he seemed to be floating around the house.

Once Mom was back in the den of our family home in a rented hospital bed, Grandma, and all the disgruntled relatives showed up on our doorstep. My sister Kim had gone and made nice to Uncle John after I cursed him out.

Vinnie's cousin Lou who he played in a band with when he first met Mom, brought his guitar and belted out one of Patty's favorites, Carole King's *Up on the Roof,* as the rest of us sang along. Joe also made sure to play the Beatles in between the live concert going on in our den.

There were about twelve relatives and friends with us by Mom's side when she passed on quicker than the doctor's predicted, just one week after that appointment while *In My Life* by the Beatles played in the background.

My frail looking Grammy wept as she held Mom's hand in those last moments. As heart wrenching it was to watch the woman who brought my mother into the world usher her out, there was a sense of peace they were together and not at odds.

Sitting outside on the front steps to get some fresh air one of my cousins frantically threw open the front door to come get me. "Hurry up Kerry, it's happening."

We knew the end was near. For over twelve hours Mom's breathing was loud and labored. She was in full "death rattle" mode as I heard it called. As her chest heaved up and down, I stood wide-eyed taking in every exhale like a sporting event not knowing which one would be her last.

Standing at the foot of the bed, I grabbed my mother's feet. "It's okay Mom. You can let go."

Up until that day, I always believed as a concept that our spirits are eternal. Our essence lives on after the body perishes. As I stood at her feet that day and her breathing ceased, I watched her life force energy leave her body out the top of her head. It looked like smoky white light, as it dissipated into the air. No longer was the eternal nature of our souls a concept to me, something that I *wanted* to believe in. Now I knew it was true.

Eleven weeks later I was sitting vigil at Gram's bedside. Having never been with a dying person before, within what felt like no time, I now had to watch my two closest people vanish before my eyes, breath by breath.

I had a feeling Gram was getting ready to check out when I visited her at her house a couple of weeks after Mom died. "Here, choose anything you want." She had egg cartons laid out on her kitchen table with all her jewelry stuffed inside them.

"But this is your best stuff Gram."

"Take it, take it. I want you to have first pick."

I wasn't with Gram when she passed, but I did make it to her house before the funeral directors removed her body. "I love you Grammy Bear." I placed one hand on her cold chest, the other was lightly touching her silver hair. As I took a step back the coroner zipped the body bag back up in a flash and whisked her out to the mini-van waiting in the driveway to take her to the funeral home. Still numb from my mother's death, I could barely cry when Grammy passed. Time seemed to move in slow motion, even halting the tears I knew were inside of me, but I couldn't release.

Driving straight to my family home I grew up in after the coroner pulled away, I was greeted by Joe at the door.

"I'm HIV positive."

Vinnie sat silently hunched over the desk he kept downstairs with a bewildered look on his face. His body posture oozed grief and sadness as I approached Joe.

"Well, *hello* to you too. Sorry to hear that."

I wasn't really sorry to hear his news. I was pissed and sorry about his timing.

Our Grandmother just died a couple of hours ago and Mom's been dead for a whopping eleven weeks. Are you trying to make me have a nervous breakdown? Couldn't you have waited a month, a week, or even a few days for us to process all this loss before you laid this on us?" I seethed silently as we stood eye to eye in the basement, hoping he could read my mind.

Feeling like I needed a major dose of oxygen, I took several deep breaths before I spoke. "I just saw Grandma hauled out of her house in a body bag Joe and I'm a bit shaken. I need some time to process this."

Gathering as much sincerity as I could, I felt a dueling energy combination welling up inside of me. While I had an overwhelming desire to punch his lights out, I also wanted to fall to the ground and weep at the absurdity this was all happening in such a short stretch of time.

Exiting quickly, I ran to my car without looking back. I didn't trust myself to resist my own urge to blurt something out in anger and make the situation even worse. I just wanted to get as far away as possible. Because of Joe's wacky behavior lately, there was a part of me that didn't even know if I believed he was telling the truth that he was HIV positive or just trying to mess with us. Meth has many psychological side effects, even when you are not using it, including being delusional. It would turn out that Joe was truly HIV positive.

After Mom and Gram passed, Joe attempted rehab several times. It would always be for a few days, and then he would sign himself out losing patience with the process of detoxing and the necessary recovery work required. Like most addicts, Joe didn't like people telling him what to do, even if it meant getting better. Eventually, he was diagnosed with bi-polar disorder and began treatment for that while he tried to get off drugs.

He always went off to rehab with a bang. Not long after Mom and Gram died, he invited me over to our family home for a special "send-off" dinner he was throwing himself.

"Hey sis, give me some sugar!" Joe greeted me at the front door like it was New Year's Eve with a big hug, looking like a cross between Elton John and Kiki Dee. His breath reeked of booze.

He had on skintight silver leggings, black eyeliner with shadow, and platform boots that made him look at least six inches taller. "Hope you are hungry!" Joe strapped on his apron and took out five small perfectly browned Cornish Game Hens from the kitchen oven.

"Who the hell cooks Cornish Game Hens and roasted Brussels sprouts, in a get up like that, the very night before they're going to rehab?" I whispered across the table to Kim, as she shrugged her shoulders in amusement. Vinnie was the last to sit down at the table and went with Joe's flow like he'd always done. He had an empty look in his eyes as he piled the perfectly browned sprouts onto his plate.

Another night in the bizarre world of Joe, I thought to myself as I cut into my moist and delicious Cornish Game Hen. *Maybe I am the crazy one,* I thought, bewildered that nobody else seemed to act like this was anything out of the ordinary.

Between the loss of Mom and Gram, and Joe's HIV announcement, I became more and more connected to the brevity of life. One night I wrote a list of things that I wanted to experience during my time on earth. At the top of the list was a loving romantic relationship. *I'll be damned if I give up on love,* I thought as I reviewed my piece of paper.

After my divorce from Danny my love life consisted mostly of booty calls. Not one-night stands, but relationships that weren't really relationships. They weren't even dating. You don't really get to know a person when they show up at your house at 4 o'clock in the morning and are gone by 7 AM.

Not that I didn't want more, I yearned for a man to love me. My underlying unconscious belief that I didn't deserve it was reflected in the quality of relationships I was attracting. Lonely and unsure of myself, I took whatever breadcrumbs I could get. For over a decade, I only dated a couple of men serious enough that I would introduce them to Matthew, and still even those were lacking in true substance.

Within two years of writing my list, I met James through mutual friends at a local pub. After about five dates, we were out to dinner when I decided to take a new tactic and not hide the shame of my past. *Love me for who I am or just leave now* became my new motto.

"Just so you know, I cheated on my first husband."

Bam! Take that. I dare you to stay…

Knowing I was under no obligation to share my history with James at this early stage of our relationship, it felt better than having the weight of worrying whether he would accept me later when he found out the truth.

Whew! I've made progress because no matter how he responds, my willingness to be seen means more than his acceptance of me.

Not looking up from his menu, James quietly thumbed through the multiple pages. "What do you want for an appetizer?"

That's it? What do I want for an appetizer? Seriously?

"Um. Shrimp cocktail sounds good."

And that was that. We married three years later. Fourteen years after my divorce from Danny. Five years after the passing of Mom and Gram.

~Chapter 9~

Transformation

What is my purpose? I scribbled in capital letters across a yellow legal sized pad repeatedly one weekend morning when James was away with his kids at a school sporting event. Married to him for three years, I now had everything I dreamed of back in the beginning days of rebuilding my life after my divorce from Danny. I had a career, a husband, two nice homes (one was an apartment in New York City), and a loving relationship with my son Matt.

And yet, there was no denying that something was still missing.

A nagging feeling that I was not being who I was meant to be in the world started to chomp at my heels. Threads of yearning streamed through me daily, except I didn't know what I was yearning for. Now in my forties, I spent more time contemplating my existence. When I allowed myself to open and feel the empty space within, fear would flow through me. I realized if I kept plodding through life like I was, perhaps I would never be a fully expressed human being doing what I was born to do in the world. This inquiry within would peel back yet another layer, inching me closer to owning my worth.

Getting easily thrown off by the fact that I didn't have any normal special talents, like singing, dancing, math, painting, or tennis, I would get caught up in believing perhaps I was the only human being born without a gift to share.

A purpose or calling does not have to automatically align with your career in this moment, I convinced myself as put my pen to paper. *Just write down everything that sets your heart on fire and let's see what you come up with.*

Three sheets of paper later, it boiled down to this: My calling is to support people to heal and grow into the best version of themselves.

How the hell am I going to do that? I thought as my clarity seemed to create a new sense of confusion.

Enrolling at Coach U, one of the largest professional coaching schools in the world, I reawakened my passion and curiosity of the human condition and what makes us tick. Devouring my classes, I began to build and assimilate new skills and loved the experience of coaching others. I was certain what I was learning would also support me in my career in electronics.

For a few years I had put the brakes on my self-development. One evening in the first few months of dating James, I found him on his hands and knees in my living room perusing my beloved bookshelf.

"Are you one of those weirdos?"

"What do you mean?" A familiar queasy feeling bubbled up within me.

"Well you know the titles of these self-help and spiritual books make you seem like you are one of those weirdos."

Not knowing what to say, I just nervously laughed and began the painful journey of shrinking back to who I once was.

Maybe no man will ever embrace your spiritual side. You may want to tuck that away. After all, relationships are about comprise, I reasoned with myself, not willing to see the truth that I was betraying my soul to fit into what someone else felt was normal. Devaluing my essential self.

Being reunited with my passion for personal development by going to coaching school, had me take even a deeper dive back in to my studies when I decided to sign up for a series of transformational workshops that several of my friends had attended with amazing results.

It would be here that I stood up at the front of the room, microphone in hand and told 148 people I was raped. Sharing my story without shame allowed me to reclaim parts of myself I deemed unacceptable. The trainer who was a woman, also shared a personal story revealing how her own lack of willingness to be vulnerable with men kept the intimacy she wanted at a distance. As she spoke, it was as if I was looking in a mirror that revealed my own armor. Weeping, I felt the true heaviness of the unnecessary weight I'd been carrying with me for so many years.

Visions of my baseball bat and scissors twirled though my head, as I made the conscious choice to let them go in that moment. Feeling lighter as I walked out of the room that day, I knew a shift occurred within that was different than anything I had ever experienced. I was still blind to the fact my inability to be vulnerable was directly connected to my lack of worth, but this was the beginning of excavating this deeply held belief buried deep within my subconscious.

It felt as if my past was shed like a snake's skin left behind to glance at if I wished. I could see the remnants of it, but it didn't weigh me down. It was just something that happened. Not because I was bad or deserving of the incidents, but because I was human. As much as we are co-creators in our lives, things happen sometimes that seem totally out of our control.

The greatest tool I let sink in was that we can reframe any circumstance. We aren't what happens to us, we are how we choose to respond to what happens to us. I had read about this concept years before and was already studying this premise in coaching school. The concept is weaved within Marianne Williamson's teachings also, however at this moment in my life I was ready to not just look at this information from an intellectual perspective, but to really allow it in on a visceral level.

WORTHY

I learned events are inherently neutral. They are just occasions that happen in a moment in time. Thinking is what changes them. *We* are the ones that assign the meaning of good or bad, right or wrong, negative or positive, life-sucking or life-enhancing, to the happenings in our lives.

The "little voice" in our head is constantly yapping and assigning meaning to everything we do, see, and experience without us even consciously realizing it most of the time. But there is good news. Even though our monkey mind is constantly in motion, we don't need to be a slave to what it has to say. *The truth is that we get to choose how we react to even the most horrific events.* Including the occurrences that would certainly give us the right to curl up in a ball and never leave our house again.

Understanding how the power of reframing could set me free, I started to tell myself new empowering stories. My chaotic childhood, my relationships with my parents, being held up at gunpoint, being raped, and the circumstances around my divorce now became events in which I could paint a new landscape and meaning if I so chose. Little by little I started to rewire my neuropathways around my beliefs about myself.

What if the worst things that happened to me, are also the best things? What would be possible if I lived from that perspective?

Starting to feel my way through life with my heart and not just from reactive response in my head, I no longer felt like a victim or a slave to my past. Becoming grateful for my history, I could even see the gifts in my mistakes.

Integrating what I learned at Coach U and the Transformational coaching I was actively participating in, I felt I was on the right track to living my calling. The niche that seemed perfectly fit for me was women's empowerment coaching. After all, we teach what we need to learn the most. Feeling certain that writing a personal development book would be the next step for me, I was excited to begin the outline.

Smack dab in the middle of coaching a leadership program, I started to get unexpected bizarre texts from Joe. Since he ended the most serious relationship of his life about a year and a half ago to a man named Doug, Joe seemed to be sinking back into his darkness.

Joe glowed when he was around Doug, almost as if a light was emanating from him from the sheer happiness he was allowing himself to experience. Designer clothes replaced the Elton John duds and the eyeliner. He also appeared to be sober which led all of us to believe he had finally conquered his demons. Whenever I was in their company, I felt immense gratitude my brother met such a special human being that called forth the greatest pieces of him. It felt like a miracle.

When Doug called to tell me Joe had stolen thousands of dollars from him, apparently to resurrect his drug problem, it felt as though the floor fell out from beneath me. I didn't want to believe that Joe could betray him that way. Most of all, I didn't want to take in the truth that his dark side was back and about to swallow him up at the rate of a boa constrictor.

The last time I spoke with Joe was three days before Kim found his body. The texts he was sending were not only to me, but to a group of people, including my son Matt who was about to leave for London for a college internship.

"Please stop copying Matt on your texts. You're upsetting him."

"I'm sorry. I understand K. I will stop."

"How are you doing?" I had to ask hearing the angst in his voice. We'd been down this path many times before. After doing drugs, the combination of coming down mixed with his depression would leave him bed ridden for days, even weeks.

"I'm going to go to a new psychiatrist to see about getting new meds."

"Glad to hear that. I will speak to you in a couple of days. Love you."

"I love you too."

And that was the last time I spoke to my brother.

"I think Joe's on drugs again," I said through the receiver later that day when I spoke to Kim. On Sunday afternoon, she decided to stop by our family home we grew up in before she hopped a ferry to Fire Island with her friends. Vinnie was at church with his fiancé Margaret after just returning from Alaska the night before. Knocking on the bedroom where she thought Joe was in his depressive "I can't get out of bed for days mode," she opened the door to find his limp cold body hanging from the attic rafters.

I thought about stopping by, but I didn't.

It's just another one of his episodes. It will pass like it always does, went through my mind several times.

After Kim's call, as I laid on my living room floor reminding myself how to breathe, I couldn't help but think, *If I didn't tell her he was on drugs again, maybe she wouldn't have stopped by the house. It could have been me that found him instead.*

And then the most painful question to be with rose as I lay with my cheek on my beige carpet. As much as I tried to push it away, it settled right in the center of my heart like a brick that kept getting heavier with every exhale.

Could I have done more to prevent this? Here I am doing all this work on myself and successfully coaching other people and I couldn't even help my own brother.

Not noticing the trauma and unworthiness tucked deep within my cells from my younger years was being shaken awake and brought to the surface for another opportunity to heal, I began the wild adventure of grieving numb to what was happening to me on a profound level.

My anxiety came in ebbs and flows. In the beginning I would get flashbacks several times a day of his body hanging in the bedroom I grew up in even though I didn't see it myself. Classic PTSD symptoms, except I wouldn't go to a therapist to get officially diagnosed until years later. The thought of having to put a voice to my pain made me feel like I would shatter. Fearing for my own life if I dared allow myself to take in the enormity of my loss, my armor went up and I kept to myself as much as possible.

One day while in New York City, I decided to take a stroll to an Ann Taylor store on Madison Avenue. Doing routine things like shopping or getting my nails done seem to pull me out of the energy of my loss if only for a while. About halfway through my walk, as I cut across Central Park, I started to feel a little woozy.

"Oh shit. Not again." I continued to make my way towards 5th Avenue. By the time I made it to the corner of 5th Avenue and 59th Street my breathing started to feel labored, as if I had just climbed 100 flights of stairs. As I waited for the sign to change at the cross walk next to The Plaza Hotel, I coached myself. *It's just anxiety. Keep going. You mustn't give into this.*

Halfway between 5th Avenue and Madison Avenue I found myself frozen like one of the statues in Central Park. I could see Madison Avenue from where I was standing, but it may as well have been in California. I couldn't move a muscle.

Doing my best to steady my breathing and rid myself of the buzzing sensation swarming around my head, I clung to the side of a skyscraper, hoping no one would notice that I was in the middle of a massive meltdown.

Breathe in. Breathe out, I urged myself as my heartbeat furiously out of my chest. I was certain that I wasn't going to make it off that street alive.

Is something wrong with me physically or am I just having the mother of all anxiety attacks? Maybe it's a nervous breakdown, I wondered as I attempted to take a step forward, but quickly jumped back, feeling like there was a force shield erected in front of me. Out of the corner of my eye, I spotted a French Bistro about ten paces away.

Okay, on three, make a run for it! Taking a deep breath, I geared up for my great escape. I decided running for cover would either bring me relief or I'd find myself sprawled out on the concrete and someone would call an ambulance to cart me away.

One…two…three! Dashing into the bistro, I made a beeline to the bar.

My hands were shaking violently as I ordered a glass of Cabernet.

Oh my God, I'm losing it, I thought as I fought back the tears, I felt rising up within me. I wanted to just melt into the barstool and make it all go away. Slowly the shaking simmered. My breathing returned to normal. I sucked down the wine, went to Ann Taylor, bought my damn blouse, and made it back home without any further incident.

Eagerly, I went for my doctor's appointment the next day and explained my symptoms. Barely in my front door from the visit, his receptionist called to tell me I was severely anemic and needed to come back immediately for more testing.

Beads of sweat formed as I imagined all the possible diseases I could have. I felt myself somehow steaming from the inside out.

"What if there's something horrible wrong with me?"

"Kerry, you're fine. You are anemic because of your period and those fibroids you have. Relax!" James snapped at me, as I tried to convince myself without much success, that he was doing his best to support me and not berate my already shattered nervous system even more.

"If the doctor thought something horrible was wrong with you, the office would have instructed you to go straight to the emergency room and not wait 'til Monday." Haphazardly, he patted my back like I was a puppy.

"Yeah, I guess that makes sense."

The test results showed that my anemia was due to iron deficiency from my heavy periods. Within a month of taking iron supplements, my hemoglobin returned to normal levels and I began feeling better, but it was an eye-opening adventure.

I felt like I couldn't take one more thing, one more loss, one more scare or I would shatter into a million pieces. My nervous system was officially on overload. Lying in bed alone a few weeks later, staring at the ceiling, I found myself utterly terrified for no apparent reason yet again.

As I continued to wrestle with my grief, James began spending more and more evenings at our New York City apartment, while I stayed alone at our Long Island condo. I told myself the time by myself was good for my healing, and I'm sure it was up to a point. It also created an abyss of loneliness and separation between me and James that compounded my despair. My marriage was unraveling as quickly as I was.

"I feel like a frigging failure." I was dismayed by the underlying anxiety that was still trailing me.

I'm acting as though I know for certain that a meteor from outer space is about to fly into my condo, and take the whole block down, me included. What gives? I guess my unease, wasn't just from the anemia, I thought as I pulled the covers up to my chin to protect myself from impending doom. I wasn't ready to face the possibility that in addition to my health issue, I was also suffering from PTSD.

After stewing in my anxiety for a few more minutes, I sat up in bed straight as an arrow. "I can't freaking go on like this! This is no way to live!" Sweat beamed up on my forehead.

So, what are you going to do about it?

Sitting in silence on the side of my bed, my feet firmly planted on the floor, my inner voice whispered in my ear. *Surrender.* Though I wasn't sure what that meant completely, it felt right to me.

Desperate to end my anxiety I got down on my knees and begged to the Universe. "I've tried everything to move through this pain, what the hell else do you want from me?"

Surrender.

Let it all be.

Do not let your grief become your identity.

We don't get over things. We acclimate. We accept. We make peace.

Stop running from your life. Lean in.

Instinctively I knew surrendering to what was didn't mean that life would be perfect or that I would forever more be untouched by challenges and tragedy if I choose to live this way. I also knew my fears wouldn't magically disappear.

"No more resisting what is, and no more denying who I truly am." I coached myself as I looked at my reflection in the mirror, realizing I let important pieces of my identity be locked away so I could better fit into a mold of what I thought other people in my life thought I should be. I was ready to live on my own terms and let go no matter what my life ended up looking like.

It took a year, but twelve months later while walking down a street in Manhattan, I whispered into the wind, "I declare I will speak at a TEDxWomen Event this December."

This was a stretch for me since I had an opposing energy mix of a deep desire to speak in public, yet tremendous fear my anxiety would rear its ugly head and make a fool of me. The anxiety kept winning up until now.

During the year I developed my own coaching practice, website, blog, and had been focusing more and more on women owning their power. I also began writing this book.

Taking a speech writing class to support myself in crafting a talk that would inspire others, I decided to swing out big and apply to several TEDxWomen events that year. After a phone interview with the curator of TEDxHobokenWomen, I was picked to be a speaker. The topic would be "Owning Your Power." Dream come true moment.

As I stood in the dark on the side of the stage as the curator was reading my bio to the audience I thought, *you can hang out here in the shadows for the rest of your life letting your fears and what has happened suck the life out of you, or you can step into the spotlight and be all you are meant to be. You can heal. Your choice.*

As the realization I would not be on that stage had Joe not taken his life washed over me, the butterflies already zipping around in my stomach started to flutter their wings even faster.

What if the worst thing that happened to me, is the best thing that happened to me? What would be possible if I lived from that perspective?

As crazy and radical as it sounds to choose the belief that my brother's suicide and my consequential breakdown was the best thing that happened to me, I knew as I stood there this perspective was my doorway out of my inner hell. Joe's death was a catalyst for transformation if I allowed it to be. And so, I took a deep breath, aligned with my worthy self, and stepped onto the stage and began my life again.

PART III

THE RISING

When we deny our stories, they define us. When we own our stories, we get to write a brave new ending.

Brené Brown

~Chapter 10~

Full Circle

A couple of significant events occurred right before I took the stage at TEDxHoboken Women.

1. I met Oprah.
2. My family followed Joe's wishes and spread his ashes.

"Additional seats available for Oprah's Lifeclass! READ AND RESPOND!" My heart immediately began to race as I stared at my email on my iPhone.

Holy Shit! I'm going to see Oprah! I've been waiting for 20 years for this moment.

Oprah has been on every vision board I've ever created since I began pasting my dreams to poster paper 15 years ago. When I learned putting our desires visually into a collage so we can intentionally become a vibrational match for what we want to experience in life truly works, I dove in headfirst. Every time I picked pictures out of magazines to remind myself and align my thoughts and feelings with the life I desired to create, at least one picture of Oprah was front and center. Always.

While I was stunned to get this latest email letting me know the tide had turned on my decade's long quest to be in her audience, I was not surprised. Even with the disappointments in the past, I always had a *knowing* that eventually it would happen. I couldn't help but wonder if my recent heartfelt choice to surrender to the universe had something to do with the manifestation of my dream.

Today is going to be a magical day. It's a turning point for me. I can feel it in my gut, I thought the morning of the taping.

Nervous energy coursed through my veins as I stared out my taxi window on the way to Radio City Music Hall in New York City. As I exited the cab, I saw my friend Jolyn who I had asked to be my guest at the taping.

"You look beautiful!" Both of us sang in unison as I ran over to hug her. We had spent the prior weekend together coaching at a weekend Leadership Workshop, so we had plenty of time to visualize and talk about the moment we were now standing in.

During the weekend, I had made a declaration in front of about 30 people that Jolyn and I would be in the first few rows of Radio City for the show *and* I would hug Oprah.

"They are letting people in, so let's get on the line." Jolyn grabbed my wrist and turned me around to join the procession of neon color clad women heading into the theater.

"Here's your ticket and put on your hot pink wristband." Handing over the sacred goods, I double checked we had everything we needed to get in as we approached the doors.

"Hi, we would like you to take a seat for the show." An usher approached us seeming to appear out of thin air. "You can come back out once you know where you are sitting." We looked at each other and shrugged our shoulders. Neither one of us had ever had an usher come up while we were wandering around taking in the sights and ask us to take our seats.

"Hell, if Oprah wants me to sit, I'll sit. Hell, I'll stand on my head if Oprah says to!" I blurted as we were escorted up to the front of the line, thinking that it seemed a little weird that they had us intentionally cut at least 50 people.

"Now, please go see that usher over there." On our third usher, this one pointed her finger towards another young woman. "Show her your wristband and she will tell you where to go."

Again, Jolyn and I looked at each other and shrugged our shoulders.

After being bounced around from usher to usher, getting closer to the stage with every pass off, we found ourselves at the front of Radio City Music Hall waiting for the producer to seat us.

"Hi ladies! I'm the producer, please follow me to your seats."

Removing the red velvet rope to let us into the VIP section, she sat us in the front row, cut off our pink bracelets with a tiny scissor and walked away like it was no big deal.

"HOLY MOTHER OF GOD!" Whispering, I was barely able to get a word out as I turned towards Jolyn and grabbed her hands. Feeling my body heat rising, I started to fan myself wildly.

"Okay, let's just sit here and take this in." Jolyn knew she was living inside a dream come true for me and provided the space to really be in the moment.

"Now I know why they always have oxygen on hand for the 'Oprah's Favorite Things' show every year. I might need some myself!"

Breathe in. Breath out, I chanted to myself trying to keep the air flowing and to remain upright. "I'm so worked up I can't even get my fingers to move to text anyone and let them know we are in the front row!"

After the producer spent a few minutes warming up the crowd by chatting with us and having us bust a few dance moves, it was time to take our seats.

I had hummingbirds flying around in my stomach in anticipation of what it would be like to see my icon in person. *Will I lose it and start bawling like a baby or act like a star struck fool?* I wondered to myself as I worked to get comfortable in my seat.

It was the early 90's when I was standing in front of my television in my living room, a 23-year old woman with her life disintegrating, watching the Oprah Winfrey Show episode when Marianne Williamson discussed her book, *A Return to Love; Reflections on a Course in Miracles.*

Sitting there staring at the stage waiting for Oprah, I recalled what I said to my younger self the day my world was rocked by the concept of choice.

All is not lost in the midst of what is occurring. Perhaps there is a way out of the darkness. Loserville isn't my guaranteed destination just because my life took a turn into the unexpected and I've made mistakes. I can and will reinvent myself.

That one hour certainly changed the course of my life forever.

Nearly twenty years later, I couldn't help but think about my journey from that moment to where I now stood. So many ups and downs. Breakdowns and breakthroughs. And now after experiencing my ultimate breakdown, I was sitting in the front row waiting to see Oprah live and in person. *Perhaps life's magic is making a comeback.*

It felt nothing short of miraculous. Painful moments included. Oprah taught me by sharing her own personal struggles with a difficult childhood and a low sense of self- worth; if she could heal, so could I.

In retrospect, I know the universe stuck me in that front row on purpose. It wasn't luck or chance. It was a divine appointment. To me, Oprah is the ultimate embodiment of what is possible when we let go of limiting beliefs and old stories and start to value ourselves and our vision for our lives. If this sacred moment didn't give me the courage to look within my soul for what was missing, what would?

It took me a while to get healing would be a choice.

Someone wasn't going to come and sprinkle magic fairy dust on me and pronounce me fully restored. The Universe wasn't going to step in and say, "This chick has endured enough, let's give her a break."

Waking up one morning with amnesia as if none of my past happened or Joe didn't die the way he did wasn't a part of the plan. Time was not healing this puppy.

This is my life. I can't rewrite history, but I can redefine myself if I choose.

As I sat there, I realized it was perfect timing for my dream to come to fruition. Finding my way around my new life without Joe and working on healing my other traumas, I was ready to step out and live my life purpose. This moment was the end of one era and all at once becoming the beginning of another.

Sitting in the front row at Oprah's Lifeclass had me buoyed up by the universe as if it was gently whispering in my ear. *There are rewards for staying the course. Don't ever give up on what you feel passionate about. Keep going, even when life gets incredibly painful and messy. Crawl on. The clouds will part, they always do. Life's magic always returns if we allow it in.*

At 43, I realized I was at a time in life where I could have more years behind me than ahead of me, and this was not the time to play it safe or small anymore. "This feels like the perfect ending of the first chapter of my life story. I've come full circle." I smiled at Jolyn as the lights dimmed in Radio City for Oprah's arrival to the stage.

Within moments, I got to cherish in person the woman that inspired and showed me that having a challenging past didn't have to lead to despair. It can lead to greatness. Like a Phoenix from the ashes, I could feel the powerful woman in me rise as I considered the past eighteen years. Somehow, I knew that I had arrived to precisely this place, the place I was meant to be.

The entire crowd went nuts when Oprah walked on stage. After a couple of minutes of cheering, we took our seats and I assured myself, *Okay, you didn't lose your marbles when you saw her.* It felt perfect.

On one of the commercial breaks Oprah was close to us and I whispered to Jolyn, "Okay sister, this is my chance."

"Oprah!" I spoke loud enough to catch her attention.

"Yes…"

"Can I give you a hug?" Holding the clear intention that she was going to come over to me, I took a deep breath.

She wiggled her way between the people sitting behind us in the second row and made her way over to give me a big squeeze. I stood there for a moment and locked eyes with her, thinking to myself, *Holy shit I'm looking directly into Oprah Winfrey's big brown beautiful eyes.* They were soulful and present. Never mind that Radio City holds over 6,000 people, I felt like we were the only two people in the theatre.

"You have been on my vision board since the beginning of time." We stood facing each other holding each other's arms, our hands resting on the other's elbows.

"I've always wanted to thank you in person for the incredible gifts you and your show have given me. Thank you, I am so grateful for this moment."

"You're welcome."

Oprah and I hugged again. This time she squeezed me a little tighter. As she released me, I started to lightly kick Jolyn's shin to break her out of her trance and take a picture.

Jolyn chimed in as she snapped away on her camera phone. "This is the result of a declaration Kerry made on Saturday night."

"Plus, the vision board of course," I added.

Oprah winked at us as she made her way out of the aisle. "People don't know how powerful they are."

~Chapter 11~

Ashes to Ashes

We rode across the Great South Bay together on the ferry as a family like we did countless times before. Vinnie, Kim, and I filed into the rows on the boat taking seats alongside each other as the captain started the engines, exactly one year and six days after the anniversary of Joe's suicide (about 6 months before I took the stage at TEDxHoboken Women).

Along for our journey to Fire Island for the day were Kim's two young boys Anthony and Michael, and Margaret (Vinnie's fiancée). James and I were spending more and more time apart and he decided to skip the trip over to the beach in lieu of work. Intellectually, I understood his choice, but there was a part of me that wished he would take a moment to look deeper inside of me and see how desperately my soul needed support from him. Exhausted from having my feelings of grief dismissed, I stopped reaching out to him in hopes of keeping the feelings of shame and rejection at bay.

As the ferry picked up speed, Vinnie pulled the grey metal suitcase he wheeled on board closer to him as if to protect it. To the casual observer it looked like he had clothes packed for a short leisurely vacation, but inside the metal suitcase on wheels were Joe's ashes.

"What is in the suitcase, Grandpa?" asked Michael.

This should be interesting, I thought.

Kim's eye bulged out of her head towards Vinnie silently screaming, *let me handle this!*

"It's one of Uncle Joe's suits honey."

One of Uncle Joe's suits? Hmm, I knew it was going to be interesting.

Kim reached out for both her boy's hands and pulled them over to the side. "We took one of Uncle Joe's suits and burnt it and now we are going to throw the ashes in the water to celebrate Uncle Joe's life."

"Cool!" Anthony responded.

Kim and I walked side by side as we continued to follow the suitcase containing our brother's remains. "They are only five- and seven-years old K. I don't want to freak them out and tell them Uncle Joe is the luggage Grandpa is pulling along. They may not get it."

"No worries here, I understand." I couldn't help but grin as I knew for sure that Joe would have immensely enjoyed the response Kim gave to her boys. It was just enough of a dose of weird to excite his zany nature.

We made our way down to the beach until we got to an isolated area close to where Kim and Joe used to catch frogs as kids. They would hold them captive in a big white bucket, then set them free on the sidewalks once dusk hit, and then watch in amusement as terrorized people tried to avoid stepping on the massive amounts of small jumping creatures.

Vinnie bent down on his knees to open the suitcase as we all stood silently observing him unhook each latch. Having never seen human ashes before, I thought Joe's remains would be as smooth as the sand we were standing on, but surprisingly they were filled with grey sharp bone fragments and what looked like maybe even a tooth or two.

"Before we begin, I picked out a few readings." Whipping out my trusty iPad, I started searching for what I had selected the prior evening. I wanted to create a ceremonial atmosphere for Joe's final *Bon Voyage*.

After reciting a couple of poems, I moved on to a blessing, "We scatter the ashes of Joseph at a beloved place, no longer bound by this world, but a part of it. No longer tied to one place, but free. Every time we feel the warm sunshine on our faces, every time we look at this bay, no matter where we are, no matter how far we travel, he will always be around us."

We stood silently in a circle with Joe's ashes smack dab in the middle of us resting inside a huge thick plastic bag, like a bonfire about to be ignited.

Glancing at my family members one by one, I noticed Vinnie wearing the gold crucifix that Joe wore daily, including the day he died. The paramedics removed it from his body, before they took him to the medical examiner's office and handed it over to Vinnie.

He held the cross in his hands as if to draw strength from it as he sat at the kitchen table a year ago. His eyes poured over Joe's suicide notes as he struggled to deal with the excruciating moment we were all living within.

"I have one more prayer." Looking through my notes, I searched for the best reading I could find to express the energy permeating from our circle.

"From the book of Matthew."

And Jesus said: Come to me, all of you who are weary and overburdened, and I will give you rest. For I am gentle and humble in heart, and you will find rest for your souls. For my yoke is easy and my burden is light.

The lump in my throat grew larger as I imagined Joe experiencing the type of peace Jesus talked about in those few words.

"That pretty much sums it up." Tears streamed down Vinnie's face as I handed him a children's plastic blue sand shovel. "You go first."

Once the ashes were sunk, we gently placed a dozen roses, one at a time, into the bay. They floated east as we stood by the shore and watched them be carried away until they traveled out of our line of sight.

I watched the last rose evaporate into the horizon. *And there we have it. It is finished.*

Vinnie was in no rush to disperse Joe's ashes, but Kim and I had a burning desire for closure. I had a secret longing to kidnap his remains, if Vinnie wasn't going to acquiesce when we came upon the first-year anniversary of Joe's death.

I could not imagine Joe fully experiencing peace if any trace of his body remained on earth. And until every ash sunk into the bay, I could not fully let go.

Deciding to stay to watch the sunset, I hugged my family members one by one as they got ready to board the ferry back to Long Island. Making my way down to a small area of beach in front of the little cabana I grew up in during the summers, I threw down a small towel I had inside my bag and took a seat facing the water.

This little patch of earth was Mom, Grandma Philly, and Joe's favorite spot, their collective happy place. It was the same spot that Joe juggled fire back in the day to entertain the residents of our small community. It was the same speck of land that while my mother lay dying, Joe rushed across the bay to gather sand, beach grass, and even a little seaweed from her favorite place on earth. He placed the arrangement at her feet in a ceramic bowl for her final days with us.

As I glanced back at the front porch of the cabana, I thought of all the moments my Mom and I spent out there looking at the bay together. Over 20 years of memories, good and bad, in that tiny little space.

A nature of truthfulness and acceptance of each other's strengths and weaknesses permeated the soul of our relationship as the years went on. We could look at each other and know what the other was feeling and thinking, as if there was an invisible umbilical cord still linking us.

A year before she died, Mom and I were sitting out back of the cabana celebrating my website being featured in a big local newspaper that day. The online community was new to me and I was excited to be sharing my first writings about spirituality.

"I may not be alive to see it, but I know you are going to go on and do great things in this world." Mom reached out and grabbed my hands. The sunshine hit her face in such a way her blue eyes glowed with an unexplainable sparkle. She looked angelic.

Though very touched and inspired, I thought it odd at the time she prefaced her encouraging words with, "I may not be alive to see it." She had been in full remission for five years and there were no signs at that moment of her cancer returning.

Now, sitting on the sand I wondered if she had some sort of premonition.

Immense gratitude filled me, realizing her choice to say the words she did that day have kept me going when I'm feeling my most challenged. Our conversation made me aware of how much words of encouragement can stay with people. So often it is an automatic reaction to share what we think is broken or wrong about people. I now make it a point daily to tell people what I think is amazing about them, with the intention my words encourage them to see their own light and greatness, like Mom did for me.

That one sentence out of all the zillions of sentences she said to me over the 33 years I got to be with her is what stuck. It was as though it was a message that came not only from her, but through her as if from another realm.

When I feel like giving up or I'm scared, I still hear her:

You are going to go on to do great things in this world.

And I dust myself off and put one foot in front of the other.

Even though you aren't here anymore I can still feel your belief in me as if you were right next to me. Thanks Mom.

Instead of judging her, I grew to embrace her humanity and have compassion for *her* life story. If I allowed the dark side of my childhood to be my focus, I would forever hear ice cubes hitting her glass at night and my parents screaming in my head.

Mom and Vinnie decided to get married in the Catholic Church a couple of years before her death. During her battle with breast cancer she decided to get an annulment from my father. Vinnie went to every single chemo treatment and test with Mom. He never left her side. And while they never lost their interesting way of communicating which always seemed abnormally loud to me, after nearly 30 years together, it appeared they found the original spark that drew them to each other. There was a beautiful grace about it.

Searching for ways beyond conventional therapy to heal my issues with my parents, through reading books and attending lectures, I was introduced to the spiritual concept that we pick our parents before we incarnate into this world. Louise Hay, Dr. Wayne Dyer, and Abraham Hicks teachings on this topic really supported me in reconciling my past.

Yes, I know this may sound far-fetched to many.

No, I have no proof this true, but then again, I have no proof it is false.

All I know is that it works for me.

Choosing to believe my soul was born into the family I for so many years begrudgingly found myself in, wiped out any residual victim mentality I had remaining. Pre-picking my family so I could best learn the spiritual lessons I am here to learn makes perfect sense to me. It makes my life make sense to me.

My soul came into this world to navigate what worthiness means to me, how to claim it for myself and support others in finding the same gift. And I needed the landscape of my childhood to be exactly as it was to walk this path.

Every little girl in the world deserves a father who adores her and teaches her what a treasure she is by the way he shows up emotionally and physically. That didn't happen for me in the classic way we are wired to think it should. And I am clear it wasn't because my father wanted to inflict pain in my soul and make me have unstable relationships with men. There was no sinister agenda, just a human being doing their best in the moment.

Now as an adult woman I am responsible for the meaning I assign to all that occurred, and from that perspective I did get something quite spectacular. A father who chose me. Vinnie didn't have to sign up for raising me by legally adopting me and being there the way he was, but he did. My childhood wasn't perfect or a fairy tale, and was quite harsh at times, but I was loved. I was seen. I was celebrated. This story feels so much better and so much more empowering.

For the longest time I wasn't sure if I could navigate the world without Mom, but here I was living, breathing, and sitting on her beloved beach nine years later finding yet another new normal after the loss of Joe. We humans are resilient creatures. Loss of any kind gives us the opportunity to give birth to something new in our lives and perhaps something even profound.

Glad as I was that I was able to grow through the first year of Joe being gone and that his ashes were now where he wanted them, I knew from prior experience that the second year after a loss can be even more challenging as the numbness of shock wears off.

Though I had made great progress and was no longer an anxious mess 24/7, I didn't want to stop at just feeling okay again. I wanted to create something extraordinary from my experience, to use it as a springboard for a full life, one that included serving others. This book was born from that desire. So was my TEDx appearance. If I could take my most painful moment and turn it into something beautiful, perhaps it would make the unbearable bearable.

Grabbing my camera from my bag, I began to snap some pictures of the idyllic setting. The horizon lit up with pink and orange hues so vibrant it was hard to feel anything but awe. The clouds' edges glowed with luminescent beams of light. Boats of all shapes and sizes drifted by me one by one.

I imagined Mom, Gram, and Joe sailing on one of those boats together, adjusting the sails as they gleefully whizzed by me as I sat on the beach waving at them from the here and now. The silent smiles we exchanged as they sailed into the setting sun told me that they were well.

Unburdened.

Free.

At peace.

Cheering me on to give life all I have to give and find beauty in everything. Most of all, encouraging me to be brave even when I'm wading through my most challenging moments.

Perhaps they knew…Claiming my worth was going to take a hell of a lot of courage.

~Chapter 12~

Worthy

Not long before James and I married, at the urging of one of my friends, I went to visit a local popular astrologer. Since everything is energy, I was always intrigued by how the moon and the stars affect us and was eager to visit this wizard of the galaxy who lived in a little pink house.

"Your relationship with James is going to be riddled with conflict." The astrologer stared me down as he lightly tapped his index finger on the table we were sitting at.

"Are you sure? Can you please look at our charts again?"

"Yes Kerry, I'm sure. It's going to be a very difficult relationship."

Screw you. I've waited a long time to remarry. Don't mess me up here buddy.

Though I dismissed his assessment of my relationship with James, chalking it up to the astrologer not being as great as everyone told me, deep inside I knew he was right. The signs were all there. Something felt off. When James handed me his credit card and gave me a budget to buy my engagement ring online without his involvement, you think I would have gotten a clue he wasn't overly excited about tying the knot.

And I walked down the aisle anyway.

Six months into our marriage, I accepted a new job in the electronics industry. I had to go away for six weeks of training in

115

Pennsylvania. Thrilled to be in my own space and just be me again, a nagging feeling inside of me made me wonder if I had made the right choice marrying James.

After I returned from my trip James and I sat down to talk. Twitching around nervously, I finally settled down into my chair. "I'm not happy. I feel suffocated. Like you are trying to control every move I make."

"Well too bad, you don't want to be a two-time loser. Do you? Suck it up."

No, I don't want to be a two-time loser.

So, I sucked it up. Throwing myself into my marriage.

To have love in your life, you must be love. So, BE love, I thought to myself as I searched my mind and heart on how to make this work.

And it did work for quite a while. We had many good moments, happy even. Yet I often felt I needed to work overtime to create the soulful connection I deeply craved. He seemed in resistance to the level of intimacy I felt was possible between us.

One night I attempted to get his attention away from the television and get into a meaningful conversation that would hopefully bring us together.

"What dreams do you have? I asked.

"I don't have any dreams."

"What? How is that possible? Everyone has a dream."

"Well, I don't."

So much for bringing us together.

Not only was I disappointed my attempt bombed, I felt a deep sadness at the realization that James didn't even seem connected to himself.

If he can't connect to himself, how can he be with me on the level that I want to experience in a relationship?

Now nearly three years after Joe's passing and 10 years into my relationship with James, I was neck deep in creating a workshop for women. The topic was the same as my TEDx talk: Own Your Power. As I worked on the curriculum, I envisioned myself at the front of the room coaching these women on how to be the most powerful version of themselves. And then it hit me.

I'm a fraud.

How can I get up and teach these women when I am out of integrity with the material, I claim to be an expert at?

Out in the world most people would look at my life and think I was killing it, but at home I wasn't owning my power. I was giving it away by the bucketful by denying my true essence.

For three years my focus was on healing my grief. Finding the gifts within the mess of tragic loss was all my shattered being could handle. And now, as I sat on my living room floor in front of my sliding glass door, staring up at my healing tree, naked of its leaves from the winter cold, I realized that up until now I hadn't been able to give any energy to the undeniable fact that my marriage was decaying by the moment.

We have nothing in common, we have different visions for our future, we don't have the same spiritual beliefs, there is no intimacy on any level, and we hardly ever see each other. Why am I married again?

My stomach muscles in a knot, my inner voice piped in again.

Because you were 38 and decided that if someone agreed to marry you perhaps the world and even you would see you as worthy. That's why.

Covering my eyes with my hands, I wanted to push this truth away. I had to face reality. I got myself into this situation, because on my unhealed wounds. There was still a wounded little girl lurking inside of me that didn't think she was worthy of an earth-shaking love. A love where you get to be your full self. A union where both messy and amazing are welcomed equally, even celebrated.

You talked yourself into this. Nice guy, nice family, maybe this is as good as it gets, perhaps your desires are unrealistic. Maybe a soulful love isn't in the cards for you. Just do it. You love him. Marry him! There's no denying James hasn't been a gem to you, but the bottom line is you pushed away what you knew to be true and now here you are in this mess.

As I sat in my living room looking up at my healing tree, replaying all the dysfunction of my relationship over and over again in my mind, I got the sudden urge to place my hands over my heart. Taking deep intentional breaths, an electrical knowing passed through me.

You are worthy.

You.

Are.

Worthy.

Taking a few more deep breaths, I allowed the warm loving sensation and the words I felt moving through my being sink into my cells.

Tears started to steam down my face uncontrollably.

I am worthy.

I.

Am.

Worthy.

What had been missing from my marriage was me. Starting that day in my living room when James was down on his knees in front of my bookshelf asking me if I was "one of those weirdos" because of my reading choices, I gave pieces of myself away to be normal, to be accepted, to be loved. Settling for breadcrumbs when it came to love was normal for me.

And here I now sat, ten years later suddenly aware that I've been living and relating to James from a place of *I'm not worthy* and the results were exasperating.

Worthiness is a choice. A way of being and moving through the world. Don't look to the outside world for evidence of your worthiness. And don't look to your past. You won't find it there. It comes from within. It's the light that glows inside that says, "I matter." Fan that flame.

Our society has worthiness wired backwards. It is not about the degrees, bank account, designer clothes, perfect body, job title, fancy house, and so on. Many people that seem to have it all, lack a true sense of worth because they are focused on sourcing their power from outside stuff. Inside they feel like shit, because the outside stuff can't be counted on and someone always has it better.

Worthiness is directly correlated with sourcing our power from within. It's knowing we are connected to divine source energy, in fact, we ARE source energy in the flesh. And when we are in the space of claiming our worthiness from the inside out, all the things and experiences we desire show up because the energy we are "being" draws like energy back into our existence.

We all have underlying conversations that play in the background of our minds that we are not conscious of. I knew from my coaching experience that most people have at least one core conversation that holds them back from experiencing what they want in life.

A core conversation is a belief we have about our self, developed most likely between the ages of 0-10. While we can develop core conversations that enhance our life, I'm talking about a core conversation that puts up barriers and causes suffering. None of us are exempt from having a limiting belief about ourselves. It's part of the human experience. A trauma happens and then being the meaning making machines we are, we make a decision about ourselves and carry it into our adulthood running around unconsciously collecting evidence that our belief is true.

The conversation can vary, but it is usually along the lines of not being good enough.

Mine clearly is I'm not worthy. And since belief is just that; a belief and not the truth, we can transform our beliefs and heal the wound.

Okay, now that I know what my core limiting conversation is, I can reverse this starting now, I thought as I closed my eyes, took a deep breath, and professed myself worthy.

Worthiness is a choice. Claim it. Own it. Embody it.

I am worthy. No evidence required.

Knowing I will forget I am worthy again at some point because it's part of the human experience. We forget who we truly are and need to find our way back to ourselves from time to time, I decided to devise a plan. Contemplating ways to immediately catch myself and flip the switch so I wouldn't need to wait ten years and find myself in a relationship where I wasn't owning my worth, I started asking myself questions.

What does unworthy feel like in my body when it creeps in?

My posture slumps. My jaw and chest get tight. I breathe from high in my chest. I feel panicky. And I get an overall feeling of wanting to shrink or disappear.

Now when you feel those feelings, don't push them away. Let them be, take a deep breath and say, "Hello Unworthy. Thanks for sharing, but you don't live here anymore." Come from your adult self and not your wounded child. You are 100% responsible for your life from this moment forward. Take another breath and declare yourself worthy. And just keep on choosing and claiming worthy over and over until it seeps into your cells that you ARE worthy.

Instantly, my posture changed so much I felt like I grew an inch. Taking a flat rock I had stored in my garage into my office, I took out a black Sharpie and wrote WORTHY on it, placing it on my desk so it would be in front of me daily. No more shrinking from my worthiness.

For the longest time, I allowed my mistakes and my painful circumstances to define me. The young girl inside of me feeling not worthy because my family was so dysfunctional. The sense of abandonment I felt from my biological father weighed me down and

I continually beat myself up for a poor choice I made as a twenty-three-year-old woman very long ago. Choosing man after man after man, and experience after experience, I gathered a shit ton of evidence that I indeed was not worthy.

Heading back into my garage, I picked a picture out of a huge plastic blue tub of me as a waitress all those years ago when I was on my own for the first time after divorcing Danny. Pressing the picture against my heart, I wanted to jump into the photo and just hold that scared young woman with tons of guilt, barely enough money for a box of macaroni and cheese, but some big dreams she would bravely continue to pursue over the years no matter what occurred.

You've done good girl, I said to myself as a huge rush of compassion and forgiveness for that young woman staring back at me from the photo washed through me that up until now, I had not allowed myself to feel.

Now how does a worthy Kerry move throughout the world? I looked at myself in the mirror. *How does she choose to dress? Work? Eat? Make love? Walk? Breathe? Pray? Speak?*

Relate to James?

And I began to move through the world with the energy of I'm worthy. Not in an entitled way, but a quiet humble way that felt very powerful.

I'm worthy and so is everyone else. Just being a living, breathing child of God makes us worthy. It is our birthright. This world would be a very different place if we all looked within to source our power.

It was obvious James felt my shift in energy immediately.

Not knowing what to do with the worthy version of me, he seemed to become a bit nervous about what was happening in our marriage. Casting off the mask I wore for so many years, pretending to be what I thought he wanted me to be, James started to look at me as if he almost didn't recognize me. While he had gone to great lengths to avoid me for quite some time both emotionally and sexually, suddenly, whenever he was in the same space with me, he started following me around the house like a puppy.

I'd hear his anthem in my head over and over as I contemplated where to go from here. *You don't want to be a two-time loser. Do you?*

I can't stay in this. It's the opposite of owning my power. It feels like I'm leading my life to keep other people happy and chucking my dreams to the curb. I must lie to him to do anything I really want to do. That's messed up!

And then all the fearful thoughts came up.

People are going to judge the shit out of you Ms. Twice Divorced.

What if you are alone the rest of your life?

You'll upset the family and your collective children.

Your nearly 45. Much different than starting over at 24. Are you out of your mind?

If you stay married, you may be miserable and be forfeiting your life, but hell at least you'll be keeping your commitment this time.

You don't want to be a two-time loser. Do you?

Sitting with my desire to end my marriage for weeks, I concluded for me it was over. I did ask James to go to therapy, but he had no desire. Clearly, owning my worth and being in this relationship, did not go together. I never had to initiate the divorce conversation because James beat me to it.

"Do you want to be married anymore?"

"No, I don't."

"You're kidding me?"

"No, I'm not kidding you."

"Do you really think you are going to get anything better than this?"

Oh yes, this is just fucking fantastic. Every woman's dream…

"James, I would rather spend the rest of my life alone, than shrink from who I am."

Saying nothing, he went downstairs in our city apartment and watched a lacrosse game. About an hour later he reemerged.

"You can't leave me. You'll be a two-time loser."

"Yes, I can and I am. And I'm a winner because I am choosing to honor myself."

Packing my bags, I walked to Penn Station to catch a train back to Long Island. Feeling like I may become air born from the sense of freedom coursing through my body, I thought for sure I may sprout some real wings and be able to fly myself home to Long Island.

Then the anger came.

The more I owned my worth, the more pissed off I was at James for not being there for me in the aftermath of Joe's death and not trying to keep us connected to each other.

You can blame him, or you can thank him for mirroring back the unhealed places inside of you, namely your sense of worthiness. And after all, you are responsible for pretending everything was okay for as long as you did. Interpretation is everything. Pick an empowering story that works for you and stick with it.

If I allowed my anger to take over, I would then be a victim. Though necessary to feel my hurt, I knew in the long run it wouldn't serve me. The way to really own my power would be to forgive him, forgive me, and let it go. We both did our best in the moment.

I decided to put all my feelings about our breakup down on paper to give me a safe space to fully express my emotions about the demise of our relationship. Then I burnt it, threw the ashes in the Great South Bay, and went home to soak in a hot Epson salt bath to suck out any lingering negativity.

And yes, people judged me.

On more than one occasion, I heard, "How could you leave him? He's such a great guy." In many ways James was a great guy, namely a wonderful dad and a compassionate friend to others. But that didn't make him a great partner for me. That I knew for sure.

If I had stayed, I was certain I would not be able to authentically be me and that felt like death. I couldn't betray my soul another minute. Leaving was the only answer for this new worthy version of myself.

Making the transition into my new life, my family was a great support.

"Mi Familia," as Joe liked to say.

Insane crazy.

Insane love.

Mi Familia.

Sending Vinnie a text almost a year after my separation from James, I wrote, "Thank you for being there for me and embracing my decision to move on with my life."

His text back included a little red heart emoticon next to his sentiment. "That's what family is for Kerry."

~Chapter 13~

My Declaration

I was not miraculously and instantaneously healed by my awaking like I had hoped. My declaration a little over a year ago on my living room floor was just the beginning of my journey to worthy. This was going to be work. Work that I now understood would most likely never be over as long as I had air in my lungs.

A few short weeks after James and I separated I dove into a new relationship. The man that came into my life seemed to instantly sense what had been missing in my marriage and within myself. It was as if he was handed a playbook on how to seduce me.

He showered me with praise, thoughtful gifts, whisked me away on trips, and took me out to extravagant dinners. The sex seemed epic at the time. He liked to have deep conversations about life. Buddha and Jesus statues sat on the altar he had in the foyer of his home. He lit candles every night and meditated. He always asked how my day was and seemed genuinely interested in my response. He cooked and cleaned. In the beginning, he was exceptional at making me feel like I mattered.

I thought I discovered the holy grail of relationships. My reward for all the suffering. It was like a Disney movie for a year before the mask came off and things got real.

I knew I was in trouble when we had our first major fight a year into the relationship. "You can't get angry at me ever. Like ever Kerry. It's too upsetting to my nervous system. It triggers my childhood issues." His facial inflections looked different than anything I have ever encountered in our time together. Unhinged even. He was unrecognizable, yet something in me knew this was the real him.

Oh boy. Prince charming has left the building.

During a phone conversation with one of my best friends, I shared with her the recent turn of events.

"He said I can never get mad at him. As in, I'm not even allowed to *use* the word angry or pissed. They need to vanish from my vocabulary."

"Oh my. Major red flag, Kerry," Liz replied. "I don't like this one bit. It sounds so controlling. Narcissist like. Who doesn't ever get angry? What kind of healthy relationship can you not disagree or challenge someone?"

In the weeks prior, I had already started googling narcissism and co-dependency. After the initial onslaught of affection and adoration, it slowly became all about him. His dreams. His needs. His childhood issues. Him. Him. Him. His energy was swallowing me whole. The line between where he ended, and I began became very blurry. I was disappearing.

But I hung in there. *Hopefully, I'm mistaken and just over-reacting. Maybe I just have commitment problems and I'm looking for something to be wrong.*

A few weeks after that first fight, we had another one as I was questioning him over the phone about his odd behavior. He went from wanting to see me every waking minute, to suddenly wanting more space. *This never ever getting angry thing isn't working for me,* I thought as he told me I was imagining things. *Yeah, right. I don't think so buddy.*

I felt like a pressure cooker about to explode. And I did. Backlash came from him as soon as I started to point out his behavior. "You won't even communicate with me," I growled into the phone one evening. There was a major energy shift happening in the relationship. Feeling him drifting away, I was haunted by the realization the person I thought I was in love with didn't really exist.

"I need a couple of days to get my head together around this," he said. A couple of days turned into twelve days of not speaking to him, other than a couple of simple texts. Twelve long days of me wracking my brain and heart around what had gone wrong.

On that twelfth day, I checked his Facebook Page. It was a Monday morning. Pictures of him and a woman were posted on his timeline. *Holy fuck.* I recognized the grin on his face and the way he wrapped his arms around her waist. He did the same thing to me.

I am not imaging things, as he would like me to believe. This is the energy shift I have been feeling.

Then I glanced at the top of the page and noticed he unfriended me. No good-bye. No official breakup. He just disappeared. With a click of a button, he deleted me from his life.

I've never spoken to him again.

Apparently breaking up with someone this way has a name. It's called ghosting and I can tell you first-hand, ghosting sucks. I thought it was something that could only happen in a casual fling, not a year-long romance. The disregard for my feelings was insulting. I found myself questioning everything in my life.

How could I have been such a poor judge of character? Do I go pound on his front door and demand an explanation or do I gather up what is left of my dignity and gracefully let it be?

Just like that I was shaken awake once again. My abandonment wounds ripped wide open. I could barely function.

Healing happens in layers. Apparently, so does a sense of worthiness. It takes a while, perhaps a lifetime to grasp the magnificence of our light and to live in such a way our life and our choices reflect it on a consistent basis

Our subconscious mind is stubborn as shit. It tests us. *Are you sure you've got this worthy thing down?*

And since life happens for us, circumstances will present themselves that will mirror back the way we are truly feeling about ourselves. My mirror told me little by little, I gave myself away. Again. After all that.

In the days that followed, all my cumulative grief spewed out of my body. Primal sobs, the type you need to stop for a bit to catch your breath so you don't suffocate yourself, would overcome my being during the two weeks I spent on my couch in my pajamas.

Not one to usually let people see me a mess, I fell so far down the abyss I had no choice. I had to call my boss to tell him what a wreck I was and request time off until I could get regroup and reasonably function.

I knew I was not just crying about this man. I was mourning it all. My brother, my marriage, everything. Finally, I felt safe enough to feel deeply again, perhaps deeper than I've ever allowed myself to feel, which infused me with hope. The weapons were down. My mask was off. Though feeling like an overwhelming heap of various emotions, I never was more myself.

My rock bottom would prove to be my rebirth.

"You really may want to consider doing some work around embodying your feminine energy," one of my girlfriends suggested one afternoon when she called to check on me.

"What do you mean? I'm about as girly as they come. Don't you think?"

"Embracing your feminine is not about how you dress or if you wear lipstick Kerry. It's about energy. You may want to take a deeper look."

Having nothing to lose at this point I started researching masculine and feminine energy in women. Masculine energy can be described as analytical, initiating, driven, controlling, and being in survival mode. Feminine energy is open, receptive, nurturing, intuitive, creative, and expressive. We all have both but tend to have a dominant energy expression.

It didn't take me long to realize being in survival mode most of my life (I always seemed to be surviving something) had me flowing masculine energy to a greater degree than my feminine. Masculine energy was my armor. My baseball bat and scissors. A way to protect the innate softness and femininity I grew too scared to reveal.

Feeling there was something to this idea of embracing my divine femininity and how it would aid in my overall healing, I started to find ways to connect with what I knew in my heart was my true essence.

Releasing my pain during my two weeks on my couch allowed me to be more in my body. I didn't realize how far away I'd gone. I read somewhere dancing helps a woman ignite her feminine essence and heal second chakra issues (money, sex, relationships, power), and be in her body powerfully. It was also very soothing for the PTSD symptoms I was still experiencing. I started dancing daily in my living room to heal myself. Drum, disco, contemporary and whatever type of music I felt connected to, had me shaking my hips in ways I never moved them in my life. I experienced myself in a new and expanded sensual way. I felt softer. And in my softness, I found beauty.

Dancing in front of a mirror, I wanted to confront myself and come face to face with all the things I had deemed not good enough. Lifting my shirt so I could see my massive stretch marks from carrying a baby all those years ago, I stared at them until I could find something beautiful about them. I did the same thing with my once perky breasts that gravity now was taking over. I breathed in the hint of lines forming around my lips and eyes. I didn't want to hide from any part of myself. Inside or out.

Then I met with a Shaman.

"Do you know what is unique about you and what you bring to relationships?" he asked.

Is this a trick question?

"Um, my ability to connect to people?" I was pretty sure I had no clue where he was going with this.

"No! My body tensed as he raised his voice. "It's your unique expression of love. No one else in the world brings what you bring. You do not value your unique expression of love. You do not own your worth!"

Bullseye. His choice of words and the way he said this truth landed deeply within me. I felt an immediate shift and clarity. As if awakened from a very deep sleep.

My heart sank as the session ended. *I'm really getting tired of this bullshit. What am I waiting for? I've been given all the awareness and tools to change the narrative of my old story.*

Suicide is the ultimate, "I don't matter" conversation. In ways, Joe and I had a lot in common. I *had* to find a way to value myself. To right this ship for the both of us.

As I continued peeling off my old masculine armor through dance, I began to end those sessions sitting on the floor in front of my full-length mirror staring deeply into my own eyes. "I love you. I choose you, you're worthy," I would say out loud over and over.

I also found practicing mindfulness and meditation supported me in connecting to my divine feminine. Part of my daily morning ritual to this day is to spend a few moments with my eyes closed connecting to source energy. Allowing it to flow through me and clear out any thoughts or feelings that do not serve me and my commitment to honor and value myself.

The feminine is sensual. It's in the here and now. It lives in the body and soul, not the mind. "What do I see, smell, touch, taste, hear and feel?" is what I ask myself when I want to immediately shift my energy. Also, being in nature, whether at the ocean or in my backyard with my feet in the grass always brings me back to my feminine and divine source energy.

Intellectually I knew I was worthy, but just knowing it wasn't cutting it anymore. I would need to *claim* it to truly change how I moved about the world and for people to energetically feel me in a different way. Most of all, for me to experience myself in a new and joyful way.

Consistently choosing to be in my feminine was healing me and connecting me to life on a level I never experienced before. My feminine felt like home. *Yes, this is where I belong. It's okay and necessary to access and flow my masculine energy to get stuff done, but being in my feminine is my authentic space. It's safe here now. I don't ever want to wander away again. It is the space where I most easily access my value and worth as a woman.*

Worthiness is not just about relationships. That's a rabbit hole we all tend to go down, because it can be the most obvious reflection of where we are at in terms of valuing ourselves. Worthiness is about the totality of our entire life. When we look not only to our relationships, but our finances, health, career choices, spiritual life, and how we choose to spend our time here on earth it is very revealing. So, I began to look deeper into all areas of my life to see what my life was mirroring back to me. *Am I finally claiming my worth?* And where the answer was no, I got to work on shifting those things.

After all my revelations, I decided to do something symbolic. I didn't just want to feel the change on the inside, I need to declare it on the outside also. I jumped in my car and did what any logical woman would do. I went to get a tattoo.

Turning into the tattoo parlor parking lot, I could see the neon sign in the window glowing in hot pink. "OPEN," it read in supersized capital letters. A few people were shuffling around inside. I'm not a huge fan of needles, but my desire to brand myself was greater than my fear so I parked my car and finished listening to the song playing on the radio.

This tattoo would be bigger than any whimsical statement I've made in the past. Like my tiny pink rose tattoo I got on my upper back after my first divorce to signify my blooming. Or the butterfly I had etched on my lower back to represent transformation after my mother's death.

This was not going to be just any old artwork. It was something bigger. Something holy. It would be a declaration of who I am. A promise I was making to myself to never ever sell out again. My plan was to place it on a spot of my body I would see daily, so there would be no running away from this statement of truth. No turning back.

Bells chimed as I walked through the door announcing my arrival. My stomach felt queasy, my hands clammy, as I glanced over to a table where a woman was getting a huge flower design imprinted on her entire leg.

A tatted-up middle-age man with black biker chaps on greeted me at the counter. Both of his arms were completely covered in ink, even his fingers. He brushed his long salt and pepper hair out of his eyes.

"Can I help you?"

I pulled a crinkled piece of white paper out of my pocketbook and placed it on the counter. My hands were shaking. "I'd like to have this word inscribed on the inside of my foot."

"Okay. I'll be back in a moment. Let me go draw up some renditions for you."

I paced back and forth in the waiting room, glancing at the wall filled with hundreds of tattoos. *Maybe I'll see something else that strikes my fancy*, I thought. But I knew that wasn't a possibility. It had to be this word. This sacred word.

"Do you like any of these?" My soon to be tattoo artist said as he placed a sheet of paper in front of me. "Wow! These are awesome, but I think this one is exactly what I'm looking for. It feels right. It's very me." I pointed to the perfectly sized one in script that stuck out to me. "Ok, great. Let's get started," my new friend said as he led me over to the table.

I took a few deep breaths. I wanted to be fully present for this moment. This wasn't just any old tattoo parlor I was in. For me it was the shrine in which I would fully step into my power, leaving my past story about myself behind.

He fired up the tattoo machine. I could feel the vibration of it as I glanced one more time at my naked left foot. I choose the left because I wanted it to be placed on the side where my heart beats.

I silently called the spirit of my brother Joseph into the room. Nearly four years had passed since his suicide. *Stand next to me*, I requested in my head as I imagined him holding my hand next to the table.

This is my silver lining Joe. The gift of this mess. I lost you, my marriage and nearly my mind, yet here I am. When everything falls apart, we have the opportunity to recreate ourselves if we choose. And I choose this word about to be tattooed on my foot to be my miracle. My great discovery about myself. It's what's been missing for me my entire life and I found it in the rubble of all places. I know this isn't something the world or other people can give me. I must claim it as my own.

Knowing Joe would appreciate my grand gesture I finished, *I know it's a little dramatic, but well, you know me. I take my healing seriously.* I could hear his hearty laugh from heaven.

A wave of gratitude moved through me. A couple of years ago it would have been hard to even imagine I would be counting my blessings for the wild ride I've been on, but as I lay on the table, I couldn't help but smile.

"Here we go," my tattoo artist said as the needle braised my skin. I felt him carve all six letters of the word deeply into my foot. In a matter of moments, it was over. Glancing down, there it was in black script letters. My one word. The energy in which I would choose to live the rest of my life embedded in my soul, cells, and now my skin.

Worthy.

There are several pictures of Joe around my house. When I really look at them, letting his eyes meet mine, it almost feels like my heart stops beating for a moment. In this silent space somewhere between life and death, I realize yet again he is really gone. That first breath after my heart stops feels more like a gasp bringing me back into the present.

Yes, this really happened. All that came before. And all that has come after. I miss him.

His soulful brown eyes.

His unforgettable laugh.

His crazy ass ways that made me feel like I was living inside a movie.

The way he loved me unconditionally.

What if the worst thing that happened to me is the best thing that happened to me? What would be possible if I lived from that perspective? I thought as I admired my new body art. My declaration. *Worthy.*

As I sat in the backyard of the home we grew up in the day Joe died and made a commitment to myself to look for the gifts within the tragedy, never would I have dreamed that I would find what has eluded me my entire life.

A sense of worthiness. That soul-crushing moment forever changed me for the better.

My dear friend Joey, who was my brother's friend before he was mine, recently sent me a text:

"Would you mind if I get a Worthy tattoo? You can say no."

"Yes!!!" I responded. "I think everyone should have a Worthy tattoo."

It feels like a miracle sometimes when I really let it soak in, this treasure that I discovered within a tragedy that nearly destroyed me. Ironically, the tragedy also saved me.

It saved me.

EPILOGUE
PARIS, FRANCE 2017

But one thing is certain. When you come out of the storm you won't be the same person who walked in. That's what this storm's all about.

Haruki Murakami

Paris, France
February 2017

Hovering at the bottom of the Daru staircase in the Louvre Museum in Paris, I glanced up to see one of the pieces of art I had been dreaming about appreciating in person. At the top of the majestic steps was The Winged Victory of Samothrace.

My eyes were fixated on this nine-foot marble Goddess. Slowly, I climbed the enormous sweeping staircase. My fingers lightly braised the gold handrail as I lingered just a bit on each step.

She has wings like every Goddess should. Poised on what is thought to be a bow of a ship, her chest is pressed firmly forward as if into the wind, evoking the energy of triumph and freedom. She's headless and is missing a few other pieces.

Estimated to have been created in Greece around the second century BC, this magnificent Goddess of Victory, also known as Nike, has been a featured treasure in the Louvre since 1884.

Although life apparently took its toll on her, the grandness of what she symbolizes has nothing to do with looks and everything to do with energy. It has nothing to do with being broken and everything to do with being whole. Her beauty comes from her imperfections and her willingness to be seen and celebrated despite them.

As I reached the statue, I placed my hand on the marble on which she stood. "What a grand display," I whispered. "What would the world be like if every woman held herself worthy of such a fabulous space? "

Slowly I breathed her in. Closing my eyes, my shoulders automatically moved back. My chest pressed forward, as if emulating this Goddess. I saw myself in her. Some bumps and bruises from life, yet ultimately embodying a sense of triumph. A deep desire to move forward and spread my wings. To feel free. Knowing I am worthy despite the pieces of me that aren't bright, shiny or perfect.

Paris was my celebration. My victory. Besides Oprah, the Eiffel Tower has been on every vision board I had ever made.

On a January evening at home, I glanced out my window to watch snow gently falling and decided I needed to do something big. Something some may deem crazy, including myself.

Sitting down on my couch, I stared at the purchase button on the travel website I had been surfing. I had picked out my flights and hotel, even my seat numbers for the plane ride. All I had to do was press purchase. If there is one thing loss has taught me, is life is meant to be lived deeply. We never know what tomorrow may bring, so we must be urgent about our dreams and the things that matter to us.

I'm going to Paris.

Alone.

The knot in my stomach tightened.

Just press the damn button!

I had spent the past two years in massive healing mode since the breakup from my year-long rebound relationship. No dating. Just a lot of being with myself. A lot of praying. Therapy. Meditation. Moon and star gazing. Sitting with my feet in the grass. Hypnotherapy. Releasing. Forgiving. Writing. Dancing. Integrating the dark and the light.

Most of all allowing it all to be without judgement.

I wanted to create a symbolic experience that communicated to myself and the universe, in no uncertain terms, I was now fully in my new life. Ready to shed the skin of my past yet wanting to take the gifts of my experiences along for my next chapter of my life.

So, I pressed the damn button.

In three weeks, I would be leaving for my first ever overseas trip on my own.

A few weeks later after my day exploring the Louvre, I took a river cruise on the Seine. We boarded the boat just before dusk. Despite the chill in the air, I grabbed my champagne that came with my ticket for the cruise and sat outside close to the bow. Slowly we moved down the river. As the sky grew darker, the City of Lights came to life.

The illumination from the bridges created a gorgeous mosaic of dancing lights on the water. We passed the Louvre, Notre Dame and my beloved Eiffel Tower. All of them sparkled in the night. My heart felt like it may burst from the fullness of life flowing through me. A child-like wonder engulfed my being. *That's the frigging Eiffel Tower. It's real and not just a pretty picture I had glued on my vision board all these years...*

I stood up by the bow and took some pictures. Whipping my cream-colored hat, I bought at a souvenir shop off my head, I let my hair flow freely in the night breeze. Again, I pressed my chest forward like the Goddess statue at the Louvre. I imagined I had wings.

I thought about the road I traveled to get here, particularly the past five years since I lost Joe and my marriage. The abyss I found myself in was so dark. So deep. So terrifying. And yet so utterly necessary to get me to this very moment on the Seine in Paris.

Tears started to fall wildly down my face.

Oh my God, I'm so happy. I'm in an authentic space of joy. I feel so grateful for it all. There is peace in my heart. I feel free. Unburdened. I'm fully present in the moment and in my body like I've never been before. It feels great to be alive.

My tears continued to flow as a smile rose from somewhere deep inside of me. I raised my hands up in the air and looked up into the night sky. It was the top of the hour and the Eiffel Tower was doing her light dance. *Look at me all living and shit!* Never could I have imagined my life would feel so beautifully sweet. Sweeter than ever. I felt so divinely taken care of.

Life happens for us, not to us.

Acknowledgments

This book has been nearly a ten-year labor of love to complete and publish. Thank you to Dr. Jennifer Manlowe, Marion Roach Smith, and Rachelle Gardner who helped me birth this book into the world at different stages of its development. I deeply appreciate your coaching, teaching me to be a better writer, and encouraging me to share my story.

Thank you to Elizabeth Barry for giving me a chance at TEDxHoboken Women and to KC Baker for coaching me to own my voice and speak from my heart.

Oprah Winfrey and Marianne Williamson have been an integral part of my journey of self-discovery. I am grateful to them for paving the way for me and countless others. The work of Brené Brown, Wayne Dyer, Abraham Hicks, Florence Shinn have also been a profound influence on me.

Thank you to Momentum Education where I started my journey of transformational workshops and Synergy Education where I completed the bulk of that work. The workshops, opportunity to coach and be a part of these communities forever changed me for the better and were instrumental to my healing and thriving.

I am deeply grateful to my friends who have nurtured and loved me no matter what. There are too many to name. You know who you are. I am so blessed to have you in my life.

I am so happy I responded to an ad in the newspaper twenty-five years ago to answer phones and enter sales orders for a distributor in the Electronics Industry. I've come a long way and have been blessed with an amazing career. Thank you to the many great leaders and mentors I have been lucky enough to know. Your belief in me and your dedication to pushing me to grow outside my comfort zone (and continue to do so!) has made all the difference. You all know who you are.

There are some people who helped me in specific and numerous ways personally and professionally that I would like to thank (in no specific order) Liz Nicklas, Jolyn Bennet, Christine Miller Beltran, Kelly Briscoe, Lynn Mary Robertson, Beverly Moskeland, Sharon Morelli, Maria Cannon, Diane Sweeney, Linda Cunningham Egan, Bob Sobolewski and Jeff Bergstein.

Much gratitude to my dear friends since childhood; Jeanene Sloane, Barbara Sinclair, Eileen Pillar, Jennifer Murtha and Jonneigh Adrion. I would not have wanted to grow up with anyone other than you.

Thank you to my family. I love you all, especially my Dad and sister Kimberly who walked through the fire with me to get to the other side.

Thank you to my son Matthew, his fiancé Oliva and their dog Bond, for loving me and bringing so much joy to my life.

And to my Michael, for loving my light and my dark.

Forever in my heart

In loving memory
Joseph Christian Cannava

November 17, 1979-July 3, 2011

National Suicide Prevention Lifeline

1-800-273-8255

145

Made in the USA
Monee, IL
11 August 2021